Baby Nosh

PLANT-BASED, GLUTEN-FREE GOODNESS FOR BABY'S FOOD SENSITIVITIES

**Jennifer Browne and
Tanya R. Loewen**

**Foreword by
Manda Aufochs Gillespie**

Good Books

New York, New York

Acknowledgments

Many amazing thanks to Abigail Gehring from Skyhorse Publishing for letting us write about a topic we bothered her a lot about. (Just for the record, we're not sorry.)

Also thanks to all of our pint-size models (and their very trusting parents): Ariya, Avery, Dominic, Grace, Kellan, Mila, Otis, and Xsenia. Sometimes you all cooperated, and sometimes you did not. It was the times you didn't that were the most fun. (Ariya—we're talking about *you*.)

Lastly, a general thanks to strong coffee (even when it's decaf, we swear it makes life better) and yummy wine, the official beverages of parents *everywhere*.

Dedication

For all those amazing moms, dads, and caregivers out there who search for ways to make childhood happy, healthy, and full of unconditional, do-anything-in-the-whole-wide-world-for-you love.

For our babies, who will *always* be babies, even when they're forty. For all the great daddies of the world.

Also for chia seeds. Honestly, we don't know what we'd do without you.

Table of Contents

Foreword

Let's face it: parenting has gotten a lot harder. The rise in childhood diseases—including severe food allergies and food sensitivities—is just one part of what makes our jobs more difficult now than when our grandmothers were raising children.

This is not the fault of parents.

Our world is simply more complex and polluted than ever before. Out of the thousands of chemicals that have made their way into our daily lives, fewer than 200 have been tested for basic human health and safety. So, while your great-grandmother didn't likely have a degree in chemistry, she didn't need it to decipher a food label, navigate a sensitive child's food allergies, or feel empowered to make a truly healthy meal for her family.

In an attempt for simplicity, many parents reach for store-bought solutions. Baby food is a perfect example. What *Baby Nosh* does so well is show parents that there is another way. Every mother already knows that it's not simple to stand in the aisle of the grocery store trying to decipher food labels and price tags and determine what food is the least likely to harm your child, deplete your pocket book, and not end up in the compost heap (or on the floor).

The recipes and information in this book make it easy for any parent to give making their own baby food a try. It only takes testing one simple recipe to see that it's a lot faster to make up some Whipped Avocado or make a Mango Teether than it is to drive to the grocery store to buy a more expensive and less healthy alternative. Once you start, you won't want to stop. Soon, you will be turning regularly to the recipes for natural remedies, where you will help calm upset bellies with Soothing Lavender Water or support your own body with Mama's Lactation Cookies.

Even if you do everything "right" as a parent, things don't always go the way we expect. I ate organic, avoided grains, sugar, and processed foods, and still my children have food sensitivities. What we can do, however, is give our children the best chance to heal and thrive given the world we live in and who they are.

Healthy eating is the foundation of this best chance, and that's the ultimate power in this book: the reminder that you as the parent are smart enough to make these decisions for your child. To help you get started, *Baby Nosh* gives you the tools you need: from information on the most important foods to buy organic, the most common allergens, and lots of recipes to make healthy, delicious options.

After reading this book, all that's needed is a dash of your own creative energy.

—Manda Aufochs Gillespie,
author of *Green Mama: Giving Your Child a Healthy Start and a Greener Future*

Jen's Introduction

If you've ever dealt with a baby with food sensitivities (and I'm guessing you have since you picked up this book), you know that having to play the guessing game as to which foods might be the offenders is exhausting. A miserable baby equals miserable parents equals a miserable home.

Between the two of us, Tanya and I have seven children and over a dozen years' experience dealing with food sensitivities. We've battled everything from gluten to dairy to meats to artificial colors to sugar to preservatives.

The idea for this book was born while we were shooting images for *The Good Living Guide to Medicinal Tea*. Tanya's sweet little boy Otis, then nine months or so, was hungry and needed to be fed. (Just for the record, Tanya also has a dog named Milo, and I strongly feel that everyone who reads this book should be privy to that information.) I offered to take over this task so Tanya could take photographs of flowers and herbs, and she agreed, handing me some sort of homemade concoction.

The baby food was definitely not store-bought stuff, and I knew Otis was very sensitive to gluten and dairy. (At her physician's suggestion, Tanya had recently tried reintroducing gluten to little Otis's diet, the consequence being an hour and a half of sleep within a thirty-six hour period.) Never one to skip eating something that looks interesting, I tasted it and was surprised—and not in the way that made me want to spit it into the sink. *Good* surprised. Like, I would have eaten it for breakfast myself!

Everyone who's ever fed a child jarred baby food with the image of the smiling tot on the label knows that kid can't really be eating the food, because let's face it: most pre-packaged baby food is pretty gross. But this food was different . . . it was *food*. Turns out, it was a homemade mixture of oats, beets, raspberries, hemp hearts, and chia seeds.

And Otis was *loving* it.

So why do we bother buying all that store-bought crap? It's essentially dead food, anyway. It's been boiled, strained, sealed, and shelved for months before your precious little person begrudgingly chokes it down. There's no nutritional value left at this point. What are we thinking? Would *we* want to eat it?

Nope.

I'm not blaming parents, by the way. At the time this sentence is being written, my daughter is six, my little dude is eight, and my man-child is fifteen (he's currently six feet two and has the hairiest legs I've ever seen—and this *will* happen to your babies, too). If I had known then what I know now about our food industry, how we're marketed to, and how many babies out there develop sensitivities that can be controlled by eating carefully chosen and prepared food, I would have executed each of their first two years a little differently. All I can do now is apply the knowledge I currently have and feed them accordingly. But YOU—you might be able to start from the very beginning, which Tanya and I both firmly believe is such a gift.

What we choose to feed our new little babies early in life can have a profound effect on their future health and well-being. By sidestepping the foods that create the greatest problems, you give your child a massive boost in both health and increased immunity while lessening the chances of them developing food allergies, asthma, hay fever, skin disorders, growth stunts, migraines, and more. By providing them with better nourishment, you create an environment in which they can thrive, and you truly give them the very best chance for optimal growth and stability.

Ironically, many foods that contribute to infantile colic, gas, stomach distress, growth impairment, behavior problems, and other health concerns are those pushed by the food industry. Dairy is undeniably correlated with childhood asthma and allergies. Refined sugar and artificial colors are deemed responsible for various behavior issues. Many preservatives found in infant formula are considered extremely toxic in larger doses, and the soy in those same formulas is almost certainly genetically modified.

The goal of this book is to educate and empower new (or not so new) parents to feed their babies a diet high in just plain *nourishment* and to reap the rewards of using foods that will help their sensitive babies; not inadvertently make those sensitivities worse. Food sensitivities don't need to be part of your child's life. It's not just some unfortunate stage to be eventually outgrown. They are preventable and controllable. Certain foods might hurt, but many foods absolutely heal.

The trick is to know which foods upset our bodies, and which ones give us life and nourishment.

If the food you're eating is alive or was alive within the last couple of days, then it will contribute to growth and health. If the food hasn't been alive for more than a week or so, it has much less to contribute. By eating fresh, whole, local, great-quality foods, you are optimizing your health in ways you can't by any other method. By removing the common offenders and learning how to formulate homemade baby foods that your child will happily gulp down without the threat of reaction, your whole family will benefit. This book will give you the tools to create simple foods that will feed your baby's *soul*.

So what are we waiting for? Let's nosh!

Theory

The Nourished Baby

WHAT IS FOOD?

This may seem like a ridiculous question, but we think it's an essential one to answer in order to fully understand our intentions behind writing this book. It will also help you make up your mind when questioning yourself about what to feed your baby (and yourself!). According to the *Merriam-Webster Online Dictionary*, food is "material consisting essentially of protein, carbohydrate, and fat used in the body of an organism to sustain growth, repair, and vital processes and to furnish energy."[i]

The last portion of that definition is what's interesting to us. When you think of boiled, salt-laden vegetables in clear jars that were prepared months before a brand-new person ingests them, do the words "sustain growth, repair, and vital processes and to furnish energy" come to mind?

Ummm . . . no.

What about commercially prepared, genetically modified, sugar-filled baby formula? Or crackers and cookies made with bleached wheat flour and GMO corn syrup? Or . . . you get the picture. It sounds like crap, right?

And crap isn't food either.

So let's talk about what *is* food! This is where we get excited to share our ideas, what we've learned (many times the hard way), and how to nourish your precious wee ones from the inside out so they glow like . . . glow sticks.

Okay, maybe not, but you get the idea.

DROPPING KNOWLEDGE (AS OPPOSED TO THE BALL, WHICH WE'VE BOTH DONE, BUT NOW WE KNOW BETTER)

Pediatricians will often advise mothers to breastfeed for one year, but that doesn't mean that your baby will *only* sustain herself on milk for that long. Around four to six months, coinciding with massive emotional, cognitive, and physical development, she'll start requiring more sustenance, including iron. Iron is a nutrient that is not easily or efficiently passed from the mother to her baby through breastmilk, so it needs to be provided in baby's very first solid foods.[ii] If your bambino is being formula fed, there is usually iron added to it already, so it's not as much of a concern.

If you pay close attention, babies often signal their need to begin eating solid food; it's usually apparent by their sudden interest in what you, your spouse, or your other children may be eating. In fact, being ogled by a little cutie with huge eyes and a wide-open mouth during mealtimes is generally a good signal that the time is right to step it up on the food front. (When they begin chewing air while you're chewing *actual* food, that's just embarrassing.)

ALLERGIES VERSUS SENSITIVITIES

We use these two terms synonymously most of the time, but there really is a huge difference between the two:

> "A true food allergy causes an immune system reaction that affects numerous organs in the body. It can cause a range of symptoms. In some cases, an allergic reaction to a food can be severe or life-threatening. In contrast, food intolerance symptoms are generally less serious and often limited to digestive problems."
>
> —The Mayo Clinic[iii]

When we think of food allergies, we think of nuts, shellfish, and other foods that can produce hives or anaphylactic reactions in people who consume them or even just come into contact with them. This book is geared more toward sensitivities—foods that make your baby overly gassy or cranky or prevent her from sleeping, due to an inflamed and angry digestive tract. Prematurely born infants are more likely to display gut sensitivities due to an underdeveloped intestinal tract at the time of birth, which is why colic is so much more prevalent in premies than in full-term tots.

Your baby doesn't need to be eating solid foods in order to display food sensitivities. If you're nursing, the foods you consume are being passed on to your baby. If your baby is formula fed, then ingredients, such as whey and casein (both cow milk proteins, but whey is fast-digesting, and casein is slow-digesting), lactose (cow milk sugar), and soy could be making her uncomfortable. You can often figure out what's bothering your little one by tweaking your own diet. The most common offenders are dairy and gluten, but it doesn't stop there.

How do you know if you might be dealing with a sensitive baby? Common symptoms include those of digestive distress (colic, reflux, unusual stools, excessive gas, and fussiness), and eczema.

ANNOYING FOOD

The foods described on the next few pages are the most common offenders for *anyone*, not just babies. If you suspect that your baby has a sensitive tummy and could benefit from eliminating these foods, then we strongly suggest you make that happen.

If you're breastfeeding, a pleasant side effect often occurs when you remove the following foods from your diet: *you* feel better, too! You'll notice that both you and your baby will feel better, sleep better, and be more wakeful in the hours you should be. You'll both also regulate your bowel movements, and your hair and skin will glow like they're supposed to. Your little one will shed her cradle cap, her hair will grow faster, and her eczema will disappear. All of these things are often attributed to a "baby stage," but they're actually by-products of your baby's health. Remember—what you eat, your baby eats.

Why not both get well together?

DAIRY

Stuff from cows might be the number one source of digestive distress in babies and adults alike. At the most basic level, consuming another animal's milk is kind of weird because that milk is made for *their* babies, not ours. Many children display signs and symptoms of asthma and ear, nose, and throat issues that are a direct immune response to the proteins and sugars found in dairy. This is the main reason for abstaining—our bodies simply can't process dairy very well. The fat to sugar to protein ratio present in cow milk is perfect for calves but not for human babies. In fact, we're the only species in the entire world who insists on consuming another animal's milk.

Let that sink in.

Also, the idea that dairy is the only source of calcium is an old, misguided one. Calcium is much more readily available and absorbable in broccoli, leafy greens, beans, organic soy, and figs.[iv] In fact, because dairy is an animal product, it creates an acidic reaction within the body that forces our bones to *leach* calcium in order to rebalance our natural pH levels. Plant-based sources like those mentioned don't do this; with these, calcium is added to our bodies, not taken away.

If you still want to offer your kiddies dairy products, we strongly suggest doing your research and only purchasing products that come from clean, humane farms that treat their food animals nicely. There is a vast difference between commercialized dairy farms (as well as family-run farms); by supporting the ones that take the time to make sure their animals are cared for and their products are of good quality (ones without added antibiotics, hormones, and dirty, unnatural feed), you will reap better health rewards for your family.

GLUTEN

Gluten is a protein found in wheat and wheat derivatives (like barley and rye) that creates the sticky, elastic texture in dough. It's ooey and gooey and delicious, but it has also become a major sensitivity for many people, including the little man who inspired us to write this book.

The recent influx of gluten-free allergy awareness has been brought about for two different reasons. The first is that testing for gluten allergy has become more common, and celiac disease, the inability to process gluten, has become more recognizable and diagnosed more easily.

The second reason involves the gradual modification of wheat itself. Barely recognizable when compared to what it looked like one hundred years ago, wheat has been altered so much that our bodies don't recognize it, and some people's bodies issue an immune response when it's ingested. Basically, it's treated as a foreign substance.

Not every person reacts in an unsavory way to gluten, but if you have a baby who's clearly displaying sensitivities to her food, we suggest eliminating all gluten from her diet to see if it makes a difference. Gluten-free flour is very easy to find (and make!) nowadays and is an ingredient we use in the recipes throughout this book.

It's really important, if your baby is diagnosed with a gluten allergy (celiac disease is typically detected through a colon biopsy and blood test), that you refrain from giving her gluten in even the tiniest of quantities. Aside from the obvious sources, gluten can be found in most salad dressings, sauces, soups, gravies, and anything baked or deep-fried. For those with celiac disease, gluten consumption can lead to long-term health complications and severe nutrient malabsorption problems.

Bottom line? If your baby is displaying an autoimmune reaction to gluten and presents symptoms like crazy gas, major constipation, intestinal pain, unexplained weight loss, or constant diarrhea, and especially if celiac disease runs in your family, inquire about getting her tested.

Capiche?

EGGS

Eggs are tricky. The whites are what most people are sensitive to; the yolks are usually (but not always) fine. What we really have a problem with are conventional eggs that come from battery-caged hens. These hens are unhealthy and mistreated, and their eggs are a product of them. Not only do we feel the eggs produced by these hens are sketchy in terms of health (or lack thereof), we also both feel ethically responsible to *not* support this type of farming.

If you wish to feed your baby egg yolks, please try to source organic, free-range eggs. The hens that produce them are permitted to walk around outdoors and graze on natural feed. Ethically and nutritionally speaking, it's the best choice. (FYI: there *are* a few recipes in this book that include free-range eggs.)

SOY

Over 90 percent of commercial soy is genetically modified. When you think of this in relation to soy-based formula or teething biscuits made with soy, it's alarming. Unless your soy product of choice is specifically labeled organic and/or certified Non-GMO, we highly recommend not feeding it to your baby. It's important to note that, to date, there are no long-term studies on the effects of genetically modified food on humans. (However, it's interesting to us that since the mass introduction of genetically modified corn in the mid-nineties, diagnosed digestive disorders have gone *through the roof*—true story.)

Aside from genetic modification, soy is simply a common allergy and sensitivity trigger. It's much more processed in the United States than it is in Asia, where mostly unfermented soy is typically consumed on a daily basis in fairly small quantities. If your baby isn't sensitive to soy, then don't worry about it—small amounts of organic soy are an excellent source of calcium and plant-based protein.

NUTS

It's typically recommended that you wait for at least a year (some pediatricians suggest even *two* years) before introducing any nut products (especially peanuts) to your baby. Nut allergy symptoms can be swift, severe, and can result in anaphylactic reactions and/or hives, which can be terrifying to deal with when it comes to such a little body. That being said, the decision is really up to you. Both of us introduced (sometimes accidentally) peanuts to our children before the age of one and were fortunate enough to avoid reactions. Because of the nut situation, we haven't included any recipes that contain peanuts but *have* included other nut products (like almond milk) in recipes for babies over the age of one year.

ADDITIVES + PRESERVATIVES

When we're talking about baby food, additives that come to mind include sugar, sodium, and artificial flavors and colors. Basically, stuff that wouldn't be in there if you were making your baby's food at home. We don't know anyone who whips out the Red 40 and adds it to their homemade cookies. Why? Because it's unnecessary. No one cares if the cookies look pink, and if you do, use beet juice instead.

Do you know what BHT stands for? What about MSG? If we told you that they were acronyms for butylated hydroxytoluene and monosodium glutamate, would that clear anything up for you? Probably not. So why are these things listed on the ingredients label of many commercially prepared baby foods?

BHT is a chemical derivative of phenol, and its purpose is to keep food from spoiling sooner than the manufacturer wants it to—it's all about shelf life. MSG is a flavor enhancer, and a popular allergen; many people are incredibly sensitive to it, and it's known to cause headaches and heart palpitations.

Bottom line? None of these extra ingredients belong in our food, let alone the first foods of babes. If it's unnecessary, you can't pronounce it, or don't know what it is or how to buy it, it's best to just steer clear.

THE PLANT-BASED BABY

Hesitant to use the terms "vegan" and "vegetarian" because of their hip-pie-dippie connotations (which we actually love) and the strict adherence to diet rules these terms imply (which we hate), we like to employ the term "plant-based" instead. The truth is, plant-based diets are extremely healthy—much healthier than the standard American diet. But it's very easy to skip some nutrients if you get into limiting foods (as we tend to do when feeding new solid food eaters), so it's important to know which nutrients are essential for growth and repair and to make sure your baby gets plenty of those.

IRON + ZINC

During the introduction of solid foods, iron and zinc are imperative but can be challenging to get into your baby if she's not eating red meat or dairy. One could argue that the quality of those nutrients aren't as amazing as when they come from plant sources anyway, but they're two minerals that need to be discussed here.

Nut butters, beans, and tofu are all fabulous sources of both iron and zinc, and the latter two should be on your radar as initial solids to introduce. The nut butters can come a little later since we want to be careful about nut allergies. Also, steamed leafy greens mixed with purées are really helpful. Spinach, in particular, is incredibly high in iron, as are lentils, kidney beans, and raisins. Chickpeas and green peas both contain adequate amounts of zinc. All of these foods are baby- and toddler-friendly and make excellent finger foods. If you're breastfeeding, make sure that *you're* eating iron- and zinc-rich foods, and if your baby is drinking formula, it usually has these minerals added to it. (Again, we're not giant formula fans because of all the added non-foods, but sometimes it's a necessity, and anyway the choice is yours, and we definitely respect that.)

VITAMIN B$_{12}$ + VITAMIN D + CALCIUM = ONE HEALTHY BABY

Once your baby has reached twelve months old, there is an added demand for vitamins B$_{12}$ and D, and calcium. Vitamin D can be found in fortified soy milk (just make sure your baby is okay with soy—no sensitivities) and can be absorbed directly through sunlight. Vitamin B$_{12}$ can be found in fortified cereals and nutritional yeast, and calcium is plentiful in green, leafy veggies, broccoli, and almonds.

OMEGA-3 FATTY ACIDS

Omega-3 fatty acids are another nutrient that is important for brain development. These can be found in ground flaxseeds and flax oil, chia seeds, kale, and walnuts.

Keep in mind that if you're not sure if your baby is receiving enough of the above nutrients, there are liquid supplements that you can give her that will help ease your concerns. When in doubt, speak to your pediatrician or a dietitian.

BENEFITS OF HOMEMADE BABY NOSH

- It's simple. Our recipes are easy to prepare. We are not the kind of moms who spend hours and hours slaving over a stove. (Okay, one of us is, but she's crazy, so she doesn't count.)

- One meal feeds many mouths. Baby eats the same foods as the rest of the family—there's no need for you to ever feel like a short-order cook. Preparing one food for your baby, then another for your toddler, then another for you and your partner is exhausting. Stop it. With the recipes we're offering you, there's absolutely no need. (Except for the purées—your older kids and spouse may not be as impressed with lentil purée as your baby will be.)

- It's healthy. These foods are genuinely nourishing. Every single ingredient is whole, plant-based, gluten-free, and teeming with nutrients that will assist in your wee one's growth.

- The cost is low. It's cheap—making your own baby food is way less expensive than buying the lower quality, prepared, quick-and-dirty versions.

- It's less wasteful. There's no extra garbage and/or recycling. No little empty jars, no plastic bags, no cardboard boxes. See? Mother Nature *wants* you to buy and use this book. Just sayin'.

- It diversifies your baby's palate. Cooking your own baby food helps to cultivate your little one's taste buds. Freely using a variety of herbs and spices will help to enrich your baby's little world and ultimately result in a less picky eater. (Theoretically. Let us know how it works out for you.)

Recipe for Edible Paint

Feeling artsy? Babies *love* edible paint! Allow your baby or toddler to go to town on a recycled canvas with as many different colors as you dare! This project works best with heavyweight paper: something that can hold up to heavy saturation and some wear and tear. (Watercolor paper or card stock is great.)

You can use the juice from beets, spinach, carrots, or cherries to get purple, green, orange, and red. Powdered turmeric or curry mixed with a few tablespoons of water produces a nice yellow color. Essentially, use anything you can think of to make various healthy, nontoxic colors. Keep in mind that both your hands and your baby's may be tie-dyed for a couple of days, but it's a small price to pay for a fun, inexpensive, safe, and healthy experience.

This paint is edible, so if your baby decides it's chow time, don't stress! That being said, it isn't exactly delicious (we've tried), and unless your baby is a hoover (like Otis), she'll probably stop noshing after the first mouthful.

Here's our recipe for this crafty art project:

INGREDIENTS: *(for each color you create)*

1 tbsp. coconut flour (it's *über* absorbent)

5 tbsp. colored, nontoxic liquid (see above)

METHOD:

1. Tape your baby's canvas to a smooth surface, such as a high chair tray or laminate floor.
2. Pour a dollop of a few colors down the center of the canvas, and let that baby go wild.
3. Take pictures.

Foods to Thrive

Get ready to ditch your preconceived notions of what exactly baby food is: we're going to blow your socks off. Out with the hundreds of tiny-ass jars, in with the food processor. Your little one is ready for solids, and we're going to help you become the best baby food maker in the entire world!

Or at least in your neighborhood.

Here's the deal: babies need the same nourishment that we do. Their bodies might *accept* jars of pale green purée, but that doesn't mean they will grow well from it. We want to give you a better understanding of what types of food your baby (and entire family) should be consuming, as opposed to what kinds often lead to dysfunctional and sensitive bellies. If you want a truly happy, healthy, optimally nourished wee one, then read on.

ORGANIC MATTERS

Although organic produce is more expensive, we definitely endorse it. The reality is that most crops are sprayed with either herbicides, pesticides, or both. Farmers who choose to produce organic crops pay heavy fees to do so, which is why their fare is more expensive. We used to be unsure about whether or not organic produce is really worth the extra buck, but after witnessing (firsthand) crop dusters and hazmat-suit-wearing farmers spraying their fields, the answer became clear pretty quickly.

Here are some brief definitions of what the term "certified organic" means in the United States:

• Organic crops: Irradiation, sewage sludge, prohibited pesticides, synthetic fertilizers, and genetically modified organisms are *not used*;

• Organic livestock: Producers meet animal health and welfare standards, abstain from using antibiotics or growth hormones, use 100 percent organic feed, and provide their animals with access to the outdoors;

• Organic multi-ingredient foods: The product contains 95 percent or more certified organic content. If the label claims that the foodstuff was made with specified organic ingredients, you can be sure that those specific ingredients have been certified organic.[v]

THE DIRTY DOZEN AND THE CLEAN FIFTEEN

If you're concerned about the additional cost of buying organic produce, then you may be interested in this: internationally respected Canadian environmentalist David Suzuki has listed what he calls the "dirty dozen and clean fifteen" on his website.[vi] Essentially, the "dirty dozen" refers to produce that is almost always sprayed and should therefore be purchased organic. The "clean fifteen" refers to produce that is often free of chemical sprays and therefore doesn't require an organic sticker. Here's what that list currently looks like:

THE DIRTY DOZEN

- Apples
- Sweet bell peppers
- Peaches
- Strawberries
- Nectarines
- Grapes
- Celery
- Spinach
- Lettuce
- Cucumbers
- Blueberries
- Potatoes

THE CLEAN FIFTEEN

- Onions
- Sweet corn
- Pineapples
- Avocados
- Cabbage
- Sweet peas
- Asparagus
- Mangoes
- Eggplants
- Kiwi
- Cantaloupes
- Sweet potatoes
- Grapefruit
- Watermelons
- Mushrooms

THE PERFECT PANTRY FOR BLISSFUL BABY FOOD

Although nutritional guidelines seem to change every couple of years, we advise you to listen to your own common sense and not be afraid to ask questions. Commercially prepared puréed meats and soggy peas are *not* what will nourish your little one. Just like your body craves quality nutrients, so does your baby's. We all run optimally on clean, whole, nutritious foods, such as fruits, vegetables, roots, beans, legumes, seeds, and whole grains. So why not keep it simple, and start your baby's slow and steady transition from breastmilk (or good quality formula) to solid foods with the following gems?

FRUIT

Teeming with antioxidants and fiber, fruit is an essential addition to your baby's daily menu. Fruit will keep her regular and hydrated, and kids love it for its natural sweetness. It's more hydrating and easily packed up and taken with you on trips when raw, but cooked fruit is great, too. In fact, we have a delicious Fall Fruit Compote recipe in the Sweet Somethings portion of this book (see page 230)!

Although grapes are traditionally fabulous snacks for kids, we left them out due to the inherent choking hazard to kids under the age of two (which is pretty much the age range this book is geared toward). It's also important to remember that any piece of fruit with a pit should never be given to your baby or toddler whole—get that pit outta there, first!

- Apples
- Apricots
- Avocados
- Bananas
- Berries
- Cherries

- Figs
- Kiwi
- Melons (all kinds)
- Peaches
- Pears
- Plums

VEGETABLES

Veggies are the absolute mainstay of anyone's diet—not just your baby's. It's so important to help cultivate your baby's sense of taste for vegetables; the larger the variety you can offer her early on, the better. Both raw and steamed veggies should be offered; just take care not to boil them to a mushy mess—all the nutrients will escape into the water, leaving a very bland, nutrient-weak result.

- Asparagus
- Bell peppers
- Broccoli
- Cauliflower
- Corn
- Eggplant
- Kale
- Spinach
- Squash (all kinds)
- Tomatoes

ROOTS

Root vegetables are extremely mineral-rich and a great form of starch. They're often sweet and contribute to a healthy digestive system. Some roots don't have to be peeled; in fact, the peel harbors a mass amount of nutrients. (Carrots and beets are two such examples.) If you wish to offer raw roots to your baby, then we suggest using a julienne peeler and giving your baby very thin strips instead of chunks.

- Beets
- Carrots
- Ginger
- Onions
- Sweet potatoes
- Yams

BEANS + LEGUMES

Beans and legumes are very high in plant-based protein, which is important to note when consuming a plant-based diet. Babies generally love noshing on beans—they're the perfect finger food!

The following steps should be taken to ensure a relatively gas-free experience for your baby, which can get uncomfortable. If the beans are canned, be sure to rinse them very, very well before offering to your baby. If you're rehydrating them from dried form, do so overnight in a bowl big enough so that the water covers the beans completely, and then add an extra cup or two of water to the top. In the morning, ditch the water, rinse them well, and then cook them

in new water until soft. While cooking, add a bay leaf, which will help make beans more digestible, and scrape off any bubbles you see as you go.

- Black beans
- Chickpeas
- Green beans
- Kidney beans
- Lentils
- Navy beans
- Peas
- Pinto beans

GRAINS

Again, grains are a super important addition to your baby's diet. No carb-free meals here! Aside from being perfect little finger foods, grains are crucial in providing energy for your little one's growing brain.

This is the part where we want to stress that there is a massive difference between white rice and brown, just as there is between white and brown bread: grains that have been altered to become more visually appealing or texturally pleasing have been stripped of their nutrients during this process. Sometimes the food manufacturer attempts a misguided effort to add some nutrients back in, but that's weird. If you can get your baby used to whole, brown, sprouted grains right away, you'll be thanking us down the road. Nutritionally speaking, they're not even comparable to anything more processed.

- Brown, sprouted rice
- Buckwheat
- Millet
- (Gluten-free) Oats
- Quinoa

NUTS + SEEDS

When to introduce nuts and seeds to your baby is totally up to you, but experts recommend waiting at least a year. Once your baby has celebrated her first birthday, nuts and seeds become a bigger part of her diet. Foods like almond flour, cashew milk, and tahini (sesame butter) can help round out your baby's list of favorite go-to foods. For choking reasons, we suggest not giving your baby whole nuts. Start her off with very small portions, and be diligent about observing her carefully for the first few days after trying a new nut or seed (especially peanuts). It's also worth mentioning that many nuts (again—

especially peanuts) are heavily sprayed with herbicide. For this reason, we definitely suggest purchasing only organic, raw nuts.

- Sesame seeds
- Pepitas (pumpkin seeds)
- Chia seeds
- Hemp hearts
- Almonds
- Cashews
- Walnuts
- Peanuts
- Pecans

HUMAN BREASTMILK + ALTERNATIVES

Obviously, breastmilk is the number one choice when it comes to hydrating your baby. It's the perfect amount of sugar, protein, fat, vitamins, and minerals for your baby—nothing compares. When breastmilk is going, going, gone, the rest of these milk substitutes will be helpful. If you know your baby is okay with soy, then you can add organic soy milk to this list, but we're leaving it out, just in case.

The best-case scenario for your baby is to be breastfed at least one year and then be hydrated with the following milk alternatives, water, and fresh-pressed juice (more on fresh-pressed juice later). As long as your baby is eating a large variety of different whole foods, there should be no need for commercial baby formula, which is typically comprised of nonessential ingredients that your baby doesn't need in her body. (Preservatives, added sugar, and other chemicals. Yadda, yadda.)

- Almond milk
- Breastmilk
- Brown rice milk
- Cashew milk
- Coconut milk
- Hemp milk

HERBS + SPICES

Herbs and spices are incredibly important not only for their role in diversifying your baby's palate but also to medicinally help your baby in so many ways. For example, mint is very good for the digestive tract, and rosemary is energy-stimulating and helps with hair and nail growth. Thyme is great for throat infections, and turmeric has been shown to minimize abnormal cell growth.

Try adding some of these superfoods to your baby's diet, and see what she thinks.

- Basil
- Chili powder
- Cilantro
- Cinnamon
- Cloves
- Mint

- Nutmeg
- Oregano
- Rosemary
- Thyme
- Turmeric

NATURAL SWEETENERS

When you look at the ingredients of commercially prepared baby food, it's shocking how much sugar is typically added to them. What's even more incredible is that often that "sugar" comes in the form of high fructose corn syrup (HFCS), which is a genetically modified, cheap sweetener that has been correlated with behavioral problems in children and metabolic disturbances (such as obesity and dementia) in *everyone*.[vii]

Yuck.

One major benefit of making your own baby's food is the control you have over these types of ingredients. It's no secret that humans love sugar—it's what our brains feed on, and it gives us energy. The right type of sugar will provide long-lasting energy that slowly wears out. The *wrong* type of sugar (like HFCS) will spike our blood sugar levels, which our body responds to by quickly producing extra insulin to combat it, which results in a hard crash that little kiddies feel *big time*.

The sweeteners below are good ones—they're natural and delicious, and our body recognizes them and therefore processes them properly. No need for panicked insulin release and no giant crash. Honey, get your sweet on with these suckers:

- Beets
- Brown rice syrup
- Carrots
- Dates
- Pure honey*

- Mangoes
- Pure maple syrup
- Pineapple
- Stevia
- Sweet potatoes

*Experts suggest waiting until your baby is about twelve months old before introducing unpasteurized honey.

Gearing Up

While we love to make homemade meals for our families, neither of us truly loves to spend hours preparing them. (We can be really good at faking it, though.) There are some seriously amazing small appliances and other necessary hardware that we use on a daily basis that make this entire process fun. Whoever invented the food processor definitely watched his mother make salsa one day and thought, "Hey—this is ridiculous!" We salute that person.

Seriously.

The following tools and gear are ones we strongly suggest you obtain, pronto. (You don't *have to*, though . . . you can work up a great right bicep by mashing hundreds of bananas manually.)

BLENDER

If you want to be able to purée an avocado in ten seconds flat, you need a blender. If you want to purée harder things, such as oats or even pomegranate seeds, we recommend a high-powered blender, like a Vitamix. Babies are all about texture, and a smooth foundation food will usually produce the best reactions from your baby. Plus, it's fast, fun, and fabulous. (We love f-words—all of them—but you'll find yourself using less four-lettered ones if you treat yourself to a great blender.)

FOOD PROCESSOR

Like a blender, a food processor is hugely helpful, especially for toddler foods. Making veggie soups and stews is a cinch when you're not chopping everything by hand—who has time for that?! You're already making your own amazing baby food. You deserve a food processor.

GLASS JARS WITH LIDS (AND OTHER STORAGE CONTAINERS)

Aside from being a current trend (you know, along with kale and long bobs), mason jars are airtight, environmentally friendly (reuse them!), and come in a variety of shapes and sizes. They make the perfect containers for baby food and other food storage because they're BPA-free and can be sanitized in piping hot temperatures. Don't recycle (or, heaven forbid, throw away) your jam and pickle jars—reuse them for your baby food!

It's also worth it to invest in about two dozen small glass storage containers. It sounds like a lot, but the goal is to make enough food (especially the purées) for at least two servings every time you do. Great storage containers will make your life easier—trust us. (We're also major advocates for using glass and stone instead of plastic, so there lies part of our obsession.)

GREAT PARING KNIFE

Here's the thing about knives: you never know how awful yours is until you use your neighbor's. Good knives are great investments! How many meals do you make every day? How many days a week do you cook? It's amazing to us that many people will readily drop 150 bucks every couple of months on hair maintenance (nothing wrong with that!) but won't replace that ten-dollar knife they bought twelve years ago from Walgreens.

Seriously, ladies and gents. Get yourself together, and go invest in a great knife.

CAST-IRON SKILLET

Because your baby is not eating red meat (which can be tough on a sensitive digestive tract) and not getting very much iron from your breastmilk, cooking in a cast-iron skillet can help increase her iron stores, with zero extra steps. Simply cook in the iron skillet instead of a stainless steel one (don't use Teflon—heating it results in the release of noxious poisonous fumes!), and your family's food will absorb a little extra iron.

METAL STEAMING BASKET

This is necessary so you can steam your baby's food and not boil it. Boiling food results in a major loss of nutrients while steaming allows for much better nutrient retention. We specify metal because we feel weird about the combination of plastic, high heat, and food. (Again, the obsession.) A metal steam basket won't leach toxic chemicals into your baby's supper, but plastic has long been rumored to do so.

ICE CUBE TRAYS

In order to be a prep pro and have lots of foundation foods ready to go at all times, you'll need to prepare the foods and freeze them in single portions in

ice cube trays. You'll want at least four. This is especially handy to do if you're working and don't have a lot of time to create different purées throughout the week. Simply make several batches on the weekend (or a day you're free), then freeze in individual ice cube–sized portions. The week will be a cinch.

GIANT FREEZER BAGS

Again, these are for frozen foundation foods. After you freeze your prepped food in trays, you'll want to pop them out and into freezer bags for simple storage and easy access. Just make sure you label them for easy identification.

STRAWS

Besides being fun, they're also necessary for your baby's smoothies and fresh-pressed juices. From about twelve months on, your baby should be able to drink from a straw (while you hold it) quite easily. You can buy the trendy paper straws just about anywhere now, but they break down really easily and quickly, so they may not be the best choice for your baby. Also, we use harder plastic straws in the recipe for Rainbow Fruit Kabobs (page 183) instead of bamboo skewers, which are far too murdery for babies to be trusted with.

PINT-SIZE SPOONS

You won't be able to feed your baby any food if you don't have spoons. Little ones are definitely preferable over adult-size cutlery for two reasons: your baby has a tiny mouth and needs a tiny spoon, and she also requires a spoon that has a rubber tip. After she gets used to eating her big-girl meals, metal-tipped spoons are totally fine—she just needs a little experience with spoon navigation to get her sensitive gums ready for a hard-edged instrument.

POPSICLE MOLDS

These can be purchased at almost any kitchen or home store, but you can also make your own. By buying plain Popsicle sticks from a craft store (or even Walmart) and using Dixie cups, you can make a pretty cute frozen treat for your little one. For babies, even ice cube trays work—these pops don't need to be big, and ice cube trays are kind of perfect.

Recipe for Hillbilly-Shop-Towel-and-Painter's-Tape Emergency Diaper

We've all experienced the horror of realizing that the diaper bag is nowhere to be found and you're miles from home. In our desperate haste to figure out how to solve these agreeably crappy situations, we've developed a DIY diaper recipe.

Yup.

INGREDIENTS:

6 segments of blue shop towel, untorn

4 segments of blue shop towel, untorn

3 feet of green painter's tape

METHOD:

1. Fold larger piece of shop towel in half and set aside.
2. Fold remaining shop towel in half, and then again into thirds, lengthwise, to create a pad.
3. Lay pad in the center of larger piece of towel and position under baby's bottom to ensure coverage from front to back.
4. Pull edges of the large towel together so material overlaps around baby's hips and waist; hold in place with Go-Go-Gadget arm.
5. Wrap painter's tape around the entire waistline of emergency diaper, ensuring tape does not come into contact with skin.
6. Drive straight home, do not pass go, do not collect two hundred dollars.

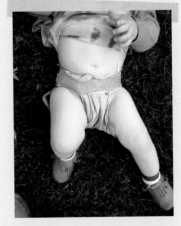

Recipes

The recipes in this section are delicious and totally appropriate for anyone in the family (aside from the foundation foods, which are pretty much full-on baby foods, even though we've eaten a bunch in secret). We may have whipped up some Carrot Swirl Pancakes with Strawberry Chia Jam for baby photo purposes, but that didn't stop us from wolfing down the leftovers ourselves.

Accompanying each recipe is a symbol that indicates the recommended age, in months, that your baby should be when being introduced to it (6+, 9+, 12+). However, in staying consistent with our opinion throughout this book, the choice is yours. Some babies are okay to eat chia seeds at seven months old; some don't like the texture until they're over a year. This first list may look like a lot, but remember, your baby will be eating purées multiple times a day, and as the saying goes, variety is the spice of life.

Ready? You got this.

TIP: Purée can be easily given to your baby on the go by using a squeeze pouch. Simply spoon purée into a plastic Ziplock bag, and when you're ready to feed your little one, snip the corner, and squeeze gently into her mouth. This method is only recommended if your wee one has no teeth; once that first tooth appears, ditch the plastic bag and swap for a rubber-tipped spoon.

Foundation Foods

Your baby is six months and wants to be fed. (Can you blame her? Can you imagine just throwing back liquid for six whole months?! Honestly, your baby's a superhero.) You know what foods are good for her, and you understand the importance of variety and quality, but what next?

Good question.

Baby's first foods are typically comprised of "foundation foods"—foods that are simple, whole, not known to cause any sensitivities, and are relatively free of overly creative ingredients. Great foundation fruits and vegetables include peas, carrots, beets, sweet potatoes, yams, squash, green beans, apples, pears, bananas, and avocados. These foods are great starter foods and are incredibly simple to prepare.

Some of the fruits and vegetables can be either blended as is, and some should be roasted or steamed, *then* blended to create a purée. Once the purées have been made, they can be poured into ice cube trays (creating individual-size portions) and frozen. Once frozen, simply pop them out, assemble into a large freezer bag, label the bag with the kind of produce it contains and the date, and you're set! If you feel fancy and want to add a little extra flavor to your creations, consider adding some cinnamon or nutmeg.

Other great plant-based, gluten-free foods that your baby can probably eat at six months (but everyone's a little different!) include oats and hemp hearts (protein-rich), soaked in unsweetened coconut milk.

Once your baby has been enjoying the more basic foundation foods for a few weeks, you can introduce her to a much larger variety that will blow her mind, like cooked strawberries, chia seeds, shredded coconut, quinoa, brown rice, cauliflower, and even free-range, cooked egg yolks. Trust your instincts, introduce slowly, and watch your baby's reactions to the foods you feed her. Remember, there are guidelines about what to feed baby and when, but you're her parent—this is your choice.

TIP: When it comes to apple varieties, generally babies prefer red over green. Granny Smith apples are typically too tart, and yellow apples, such as Golden Delicious, are very high in (naturally occurring) sugar. Red Delicious aren't as great for heating, as the texture becomes mealy and bland. For all of the above reasons, we like to make baby food with organic Pink Lady, Macintosh, Gala, Fuji, and Spartan apples. You don't have to limit yourself to these five, but they're our faves.

Bananas in Pajamas (6+)

Bananas are a perfect first food. They're soft and flavorful and full of potassium and fabulous vitamins for your growing wee one. They're also very easy to take on an outing (just mash well with a fork, if you're away from the kitchen).

INGREDIENTS:

1 ripe banana

Tiny pinch of cinnamon

METHOD:

1. Place both ingredients in blender and purée until smooth.
2. If you want to thin it out a bit, add a little water or breastmilk and stir.

Whipped Avocado (6+)

Avocados make wonderful baby food because they're naturally creamy in texture. They also contain a lot of good fat, which is essential for your growing baby (particularly if your baby is slow to gain weight).

INGREDIENTS:

2 ripe avocados

2 tbsp. coconut milk or breastmilk

METHOD:

1. Slice avocado in half lengthwise and remove pit.
2. Turn each half flesh side-down and squeeze meat into a blender.
3. Add milk and purée until smooth.

Apple Cinnamon (6+)

Everybody loves the apple-cinnamon combo, and your baby will, too. See tips for choosing apples on page 51.

INGREDIENTS:

2 organic red apples

Tiny dash cinnamon

METHOD:

1. Peel, core, and chop your apples.
2. Place in small pot with ¼ cup of water.
3. Stew on the stove, stirring every now and then for 20–30 minutes.
4. Remove from heat and set aside to cool to room temperature.
5. Place stewed apples and cinnamon in a blender and purée until smooth.

Purely Pear (6+)

This super simple purée recipe is very similar to the apple one, but we pair pear with cardamom instead of cinnamon.

INGREDIENTS:

2 ripe Bartlett pears

Tiny pinch cardamom

METHOD:

1. Peel, core, and cut pears into chunks.
2. Bring about 2–3 inches of water to a boil in a small saucepan.
3. Place pear chunks in a metal steamer basket and place over pan.
4. Steam for about 10 minutes, then remove the basket from the pan and let pears cool until just warm.
5. Place pears and cardamom in blender and blend until smooth. (Add a little bit of water, if needed, to get the desired consistency.)
6. Let cool completely, then serve.

Glorious Greens (6+)

We thought we'd throw this one in for fun. It's completely possible that your baby can eat and enjoy this at six months old, but we urge you to try giving her banana, kiwi, and avocado as individual purées first, then after you've observed no reactions, make this yummy stuff. Her mind will be blown. (Hopefully not her diaper.)

INGREDIENTS:

1 banana

1 kiwi

1 leaf kale

½ avocado

METHOD:

Combine all ingredients in blender and blend until smooth.

Goodness Bowl (6+)

Bowls like this should be given to your baby after each of the ingredients have been introduced to her individually to reduce the risk of a reaction. Once your baby has tried a variety of foods, you can start playing with all sorts of combinations to create a delicious variety.

INGREDIENTS:

½ cup roasted beets (page 149)

¼ cup fresh blueberries

¼ carrot, peeled, chopped, and steamed

1 handful fresh raspberries

1 tbsp. extra virgin olive oil

1 apple, peeled, cored, chopped, and cooked

1 tbsp. chia seeds

1 tbsp. hemp hearts

3 tbsp. gluten-free rolled oats, or Oat Infant Cereal (page 86)

Unsweetened coconut milk, or breastmilk for thinning if necessary

METHOD:

1. Combine all ingredients in blender; thin with breastmilk or coconut milk if needed.
2. Blend until smooth.

Sweet Potato Sweetness (6+)

Sweet potatoes are naturally sweet (hence the name), so nothing needs to be added to this awesomely delicious purée.

INGREDIENTS:

1 large sweet potato

METHOD:

1. Preheat oven to 350°F.
2. Peel sweet potato and cut into chunks.
3. Spread across cookie sheet lined with parchment paper.
4. Bake in oven until tender, around 30 minutes, depending on the size of pieces.
5. Allow to cool and blend in blender until smooth.

Yummy Yams (6+)

Yams and sweet potatoes contain far more nutrients than regular potatoes do. Therefore, we definitely recommend feeding them to your baby, instead of russets.

INGREDIENTS:

1 large yam

METHOD:

1. Preheat oven to 400°F.
2. Scrub the yam and pierce it with a sharp knife about 10 times.
3. Wrap in foil, then put it in a dish, and place in oven. Cook for about 50 minutes or until yam is completely tender.
4. Remove from oven and foil and let sit for 10 minutes.
5. Slice yam down the middle lengthwise and peel off skin.
6. Place the flesh in a blender and blend until smooth.
7. Remove and serve once cool enough for your baby.

Lucky Lentils (6+)

Lentils are high in protein and fiber, which is great for a growing baby. (Especially if your baby is eating a 100 percent plant-based diet.)

INGREDIENTS:

1 cup dried red lentils

2 tbsp. vegetable broth (no added salt)

METHOD:

1. Rinse lentils very well (this is important).
2. Place in small saucepan and add just enough water to cover.
3. Simmer about 20 minutes or until lentils are tender.
4. Remove from water, strain, and rinse well again.
5. Place lentils in blender and add broth.
6. Blend until smooth and serve!

Butternut Squash (6+)

This squash is sweet and delicious—your baby will love it. It's one of our fave purées.

INGREDIENTS:

1 butternut squash

METHOD:

1. Preheat oven to 350°F.
2. Pierce butternut squash 4 or 5 times with knife and pop into oven in oven-safe dish.
3. Bake until tender, at least 45 minutes or more, depending on the size of your squash.
4. Allow to cool to room temperature before slicing open and removing the seedy stuff.
5. Spoon meat away from the tough outer skin and place into blender.
6. Blend until smooth.

Sweet Pea (6+)

This simple foundation recipe is very yummy when peas are in season.

INGREDIENTS:

1 cup fresh peas

METHOD:

1. Steam peas for about 2 minutes or until bright green.
2. Throw in blender (gently) and blend until smooth.

Peachy Keen (6+)

Peaches are right up there with apples and pears in regard to most babies' favorite first fruits. They're mellow and yellow and delicious and incredible when in season.

INGREDIENTS:

2 ripe peaches

Tiny dash of ground cloves

METHOD:

1. Peel the peaches, slice in half, and remove pit.
2. Slice the fruit and drop into small pot.
3. Add 2 tbsp. water and stew over medium heat for about 10 minutes.
4. Removed from stove and let cool to room temperature.
5. Place cooled peaches and cloves in blender and blend until smooth.

Does This Purée Sound Acorny? (6+)

We couldn't resist.

INGREDIENTS:

1 acorn squash

Sprinkle of pumpkin pie spice

METHOD:

1. Preheat oven to 350°F.
2. Cut squash in half, remove seeds and extra goopy stuff.
3. Sprinkle meaty side lightly with pumpkin pie seasoning.
4. Place cleaned halves in oven-safe dish, cut side down, with a little bit of water—about one inch deep.
5. Bake in oven for 45 minutes or until soft.
6. Remove from heat, allowing to cool to room temperature.
7. Scrape contents of squash from outer skin and spoon into blender, blending on high until smooth, about 3 minutes.
8. Thin with leftover cooking water or breastmilk.

Basic Carrot (6+)

Dog-ear the corner of this page—this is a purée you will revisit time and time again. When your baby grows into a toddler, carrot purée is super easy to hide in a variety of pasta dishes for a sweet boost of vitamin A and beta-carotene. If you need to thin the purée, add a little remaining cooking water or breast-milk while blending.

As with the Sweet Pea recipe, this one is even more delicious if the carrots are fresh and in season.

INGREDIENTS:

4 large carrots

METHOD:

1. Wash and peel carrots and cut into large chunks.
2. Place carrots into steamer basket or medium saucepan with an inch or two of water and steam or cook until tender (about 20 minutes).
3. Remove from heat and allow to cool.
4. Blend until smooth.

Coconut Carrot Citrus (9+)

For this super tasty blend (seriously, our big kids ask us to make this), you can use fresh carrots, or you can pop a cube or two out of your handy-dandy ice cube trays, thaw it, and throw that in instead. (Hooray for small sanity savers!)

There are two ways you can work with the oats: you can stir in dry oats and allow them to soak up all that moisture overnight in the fridge, or you can add a spoonful of pre-moistened overnight oats. Be sure that you have introduced each of these foods to your baby as singles prior to offering her this dish.

INGREDIENTS:

1 carrot

1 generous spoonful of gluten-free rolled oats or about 3 tbsp. Breezy Morning Overnight Oats (page 101)

1 navel orange

1 tbsp. coconut milk yogurt

METHOD:

1. Remove peel from orange using knife, removing as much of the pith (the soft white layer between the peel and the flesh) as possible.
2. Cut the fruit into chunks, discarding the white center piece (watch for seeds!).
3. Combine carrot, orange, and coconut yogurt in blender and blend until smooth.

Blueberry Bliss (6+)

This purée is delish with a dollop of coconut milk yogurt or chia pudding. Just a heads-up: blueberries are loaded with fiber, so unless you're passionate about frequent diaper changes, don't overdo this yummy blend.

INGREDIENTS:

1 cup blueberries

METHOD:

1. Wash berries well and strain excess water off.
2. Toss them into a medium saucepan and simmer on low until warm (this helps with the consistency of the purée).
3. Remove from heat and place in blender, blending until very smooth.
4. Before serving, allow to cool to room temperature.

Big Red (6+)

(AKA: Old Faithful.) Even on Otis's worst days, he always gobbled up this purée. Additionally, this recipe was the one that helped to inspire this book.

INGREDIENTS:

½ roasted beet (page 149)

½ banana

¼ cup fresh raspberries

1 apple, peeled, cored, and stewed until soft

1 tbsp. coconut or soy yogurt

1 tsp. hemp hearts

METHOD:

1. Combine all ingredients in blender and purée until smooth.
2. Top with a dollop of coconut or soy yogurt and sprinkle with hemp hearts.

Blackberry Kale Apple (6+)

This purée should be given after your baby has had both apples and blackberries on their own.

INGREDIENTS:

1 apple (we prefer Pink Lady because of the slight tartness)

1 medium-size kale leaf

½ cup blackberries

METHOD:

1. Peel and core apple and chop into pieces. (The smaller the pieces, the faster they cook.)
2. Simmer with a bit of water until soft when pierced with a fork.
3. Remove from heat, allow to cool slightly, and spoon into blender.
4. Wash kale and blackberries well and add to blender.
5. Mix all three ingredients until you have a nice, even texture. If necessary, thin with a little breastmilk or leftover cooking water.
6. Sprinkle lightly with hemp hearts and chia seeds.

Curried Carrot and Butternut Squash (12+)

This great purée goes one step further than basic carrot or butternut by intro-ducing masala spice.

INGREDIENTS:

½ cup raw butternut squash, peeled and chopped

2 carrots

¼ tsp. masala spice

½ tbsp. extra virgin olive oil

Pinch sea salt

METHOD:

1. Preheat oven to 350°F.
2. Pierce butternut squash 4 or 5 times with knife and pop into oven in oven-safe dish.
3. Bake until tender, at least 45 minutes or more, depending on the size of your squash.
4. While squash is baking, peel and chop carrots into pieces and steam until soft but not mushy.
5. Place in blender to wait for squash.
6. Once squash is done, allow to cool to room temperature before slicing open and removing the seedy stuff.
7. Spoon meat away from the tough outer skin and place into blender with the carrots.
8. Add masala spice, olive oil, and a pinch of sea salt to the blender contents.
9. Whip it, whip it good.

Banana Ginger Pear (6+)

This one is easy-peasy, has little mess, and almost zero prep—just what the doctor ordered! We won't lie, we've totally noshed on this one ourselves.

INGREDIENTS:

1 banana

1 Bartlett pear

1 thumb ginger

METHOD:

1. Grab your blender and toss in the peeled banana and peeled and cored pear, and grate some fresh ginger right into the mix.

2. Purée all three ingredients together until smooth.

3. As always, you can thin your bambino's food with a little breastmilk or water if necessary.

> TIP: We don't have anything fancy for grating ginger; we just use the super fine side of our cheese graters because, honestly, if we acquire any more teeny tiny kitchen gadgets that we hardly use, our heads might explode.

Strawberry Avocado Smash (6+)

Avocado pit removal can be done easily by hitting the pit carefully in the center with the cutting edge of a sharp kitchen knife. The knife will stick in the pit, and with a few wriggles, it should pop right out, making it a breeze to spoon out the contents of the fruit. On occasion, we've encountered stubborn avocados, which is a similar experience to getting that one lonely grocery cart with the wayward wheel. You can be the best pit puller in all the land, but if you get this particular piece of produce, you will have little hope for a clean exit. Just do your best, and remember, your baby thinks you're the best baby food maker ever.

INGREDIENTS:

½ avocado, pit and peel removed

6 plump strawberries

METHOD:

Remove the greens from the strawberries, wash thoroughly, and combine with avocado in blender for a smooth purée. (For babies who like more texture, you can chop the strawberries into small pieces, and use a fork to smash them together with the avocado.)

Savory Potato Lentil Parsnip (9+)

Ready for this one? We're getting a little Baron von Fancy this time.

INGREDIENTS:

1 white potato

1 parsnip

1 tsp. olive oil

1 tbsp. finely chopped shallots

4 tbsp. dried red lentils, rinsed

1 apple

METHOD:

1. Preheat oven to 350°F.
2. Peel and chop potato and parsnip, sprinkle with olive oil and shallots, wrap in foil, and pop into the oven, baking 25 minutes, or until soft.
3. While those are baking, place lentils into small saucepan with enough water to cover.
4. Bring to boil and reduce heat, simmering on low until lentils are soft. (Keep an eye on these while simmering, as you may need to add a bit more water as they cook; they tend to absorb a lot of moisture because lentils are greedy like that.)
5. Set aside and allow to cool to room temperature.
6. Peel and core apple, cut to bite-size pieces, and place into small saucepan with a few tablespoons of water.
7. Poach apples with water on low until soft. (Cooking enhances the sweetness and the apple will balance the somewhat spicy parsnip.)
8. Combine potato, parsnips, shallots, and apples (and a little bit of their cooking water) in blender and purée until smooth. Thin with breastmilk or water, if necessary.
9. Now stir in the cooked lentils, leaving them whole for a combination of beautiful flavors and textures. You can get extra snazzy points by sprinkling everything with a little ground flaxseed before serving with a spoon to your healthy little foodie-in-training.

Hearty Carrot Lentil Potato (9+)

Give this one to your baby after giving her each veggie on its own first. She'll love the creamy and flavorful result of this purée.

INGREDIENTS:

1 red potato

1 carrot

3 tbsp. dried red lentils, rinsed

½ cup unsweetened coconut milk

Pinch of sea salt

1 tsp. finely chopped fresh basil

METHOD:

1. Cut potato and carrot into small pieces and combine in saucepan with lentils and coconut milk.
2. Simmer, covered, on medium-low until potatoes, carrots, and lentils are just soft.
3. Remove from heat, allowing to cool before throwing contents into blender, and combine on the chop setting. (If your blender doesn't have settings, you can always use a little elbow grease, smashing everything in a bowl with a fork.)
4. Stir in finely chopped basil, add a pinch of sea salt, and serve with a spoon.
5. basil

Pears, YAM! (6+)

This foundation food goes a little further by incorporating chia seeds and hemp hearts into the mix. Different than some of the other recipes that contain these two ingredients, this one should be fully mixed instead of simply garnishing the top, so the seeds and hemp can soak in the mixture and have the chance to soften before your baby eats it.

INGREDIENTS:

1 medium yam

2 pears

2 tbsp. chia seeds

2 tbsp. hemp hearts

METHOD:

1. Preheat oven to 350°F.
2. Cut yam lengthwise, wrap in foil, and bake for 40 minutes or until very soft.
3. While your yam is cooling, peel and core pears.
4. Purée yam, pears, chia seeds, and hemp hearts together in blender until smooth.
5. Serve with spoon or from a squeeze pouch if you're on the go.

Oat Infant Cereal (6+)

Not exactly a recipe but an easy how-to if you want to make your own oat-based infant cereal. As your baby's tastes mature, you can add a teaspoon or so of ground cinnamon and some chopped raisins to your oats before blending.

INGREDIENTS:

2 cups gluten-free steel-cut oats

METHOD:

1. Measure dry oats directly into blender and blend on low or chop setting until it has a very fine texture.
2. Store in airtight glass container.

Green Potatoes (6+)

Typically green potatoes are not fit for consumption, but we make this recipe green on purpose by using peas. (When potatoes turn green, they contain extra amounts of an ingredient called solanine, which can be extremely toxic in even small amounts.)[viii] The potatoes you cook with should never be green under the skin.

INGREDIENTS:

1 white potato

1 tbsp. extra virgin olive oil

Sea salt

Pepper

¼ cup green peas

METHOD:

1. Preheat oven to 350°F.
2. Peel and chop potato, drizzle with oil, sprinkle with salt and pepper, and bake until soft, about 40 minutes.
3. Steam peas and toss into blender, along with potatoes, and purée.
4. Thin with some breastmilk or unsweetened coconut milk.
5. peas

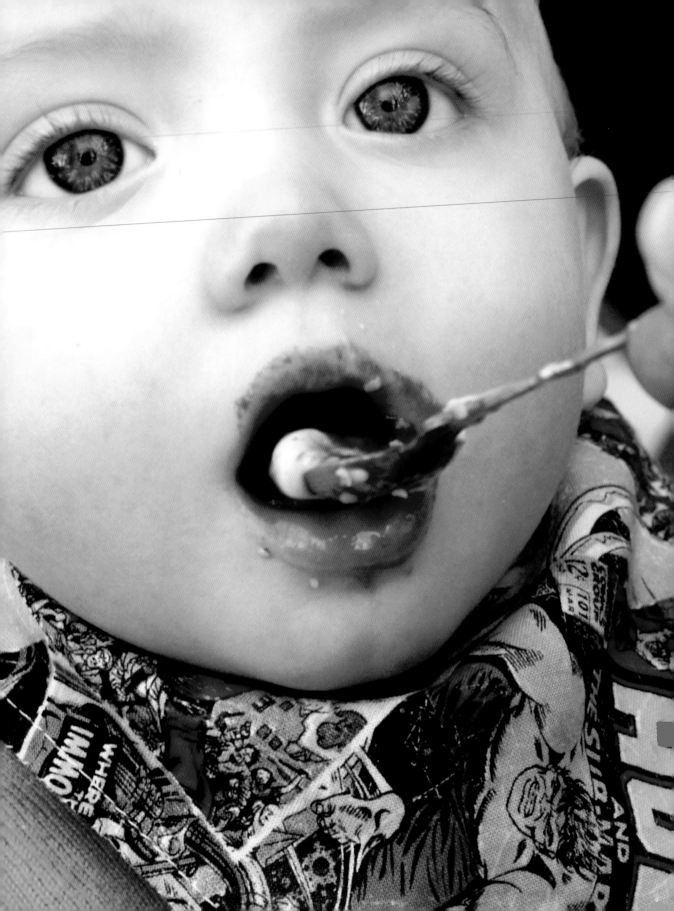

CH-CH-CH-Cherry Bomb (6+)

Make sure your baby wears a giant bib with this one—cherries are sneaky and stainy. (Ironically, two of the most common qualities of every amazing food on this planet.)

INGREDIENTS:

1 sweet potato

½ cup pitted fresh cherries

1 tbsp. ground flaxseed

Coconut milk yogurt

METHOD:

1. Preheat oven to 350°F.
2. Cut sweet potato lengthwise, wrap in foil, and bake until soft, about 40 minutes.
3. Allow to cool to room temperature and scoop inside of sweet potato into blender.
4. Add cherries and flax and purée until smooth.
5. Top with a dollop of coconut milk yogurt and serve with a spoon.
6. Coconut milk yogurt

Aloha Avocado with Pineapple and Banana (6+)

Get tropical and summery with this yummy purée. Raw pineapple is acidic, so be sure to watch for red, rashy patches around the mouth (indicating sensitivity to the acid in the pineapple), and excess gas (another common side effect of acidic foods).

Also, take care to ensure the seeds and hemp are softened in the mixture before serving to a six-month-old; older babies don't mind the texture variations as much as younger ones.

INGREDIENTS:

½ avocado

1 banana

¼ cup pineapple

1 tsp. chia seeds

1 tbsp. hemp hearts

METHOD:

1. Slice avocado lengthwise, remove pit, and scoop fruit into blender.
2. Add peeled banana, pineapple, and chia seeds.
3. Purée until velvety.
4. Sprinkle with hemp hearts and serve. Your baby will say "mahalo."

Friendly Prunes (6+)

This recipe is great year-round but especially in the fall when we are already making trips to the pumpkin patch. Fresh pumpkin can be substituted for canned, by peeling, removing seeds, quartering the meat, roasting in the oven at 350°F. for 45 minutes, then puréeing in a blender.

When pumpkins are not in season, you can pick up canned pumpkin at your local grocers; just make sure you check the label, and get PURE pumpkin—no added sugars or preservatives, and organic if possible. Also, look for BPA-free cans.

INGREDIENTS:

½ cup pure pumpkin purée

2 pitted prunes

½ cup coconut milk yogurt or soy yogurt

1 tbsp. pure maple syrup (optional)

METHOD:

1. Throw pumpkin, prunes, yogurt, and maple syrup (optional) into blender and whirl on medium until prunes are completely puréed and all ingredients are combined.
2. Serve.

Broc-O-Baby Greenies (9+)

This purée is high on the vitamin and antioxidant charts but may bother a baby susceptible to excess gas. If your baby falls into this category, skip the broccoli for now.

INGREDIENTS:

¼ cup broccoli

¼ cup green beans

2 pears

METHOD:

1. Cut broccoli and beans into pieces.
2. Place veggies in steamer basket and steam until bright green and soft. Allow to cool.
3. While veggies are cooling, peel and core pears.
4. Add broccoli, beans, and pears to blender and purée, thinning with breast-milk or water if necessary.

Sweet Carrot Velvet with Raspberry and Apricot (6+)

This foundation food is lovely. Be sure to introduce each ingredient individually ahead of time.

INGREDIENTS:

1 carrot

¼ cup raspberries

2 apricots

METHOD:

1. Peel and chop carrot into two-inch chunks and place in steamer basket.

2. Steam carrot until just soft and bright orange.

3. Combine carrot, raspberries, and apricots into blender and purée until everything has an even consistency.

Cherry Squash (6+)

This purée is soft enough that your baby can easily enjoy it off of a spoon or from a squeeze pouch.

INGREDIENTS:

1 small butternut squash

½ cup pitted fresh cherries

1 tbsp. ground flaxseeds

METHOD:

1. Preheat oven to 350°F.
2. Pierce butternut squash 4 or 5 times with knife and pop into oven in oven-safe dish.
3. Bake until tender, at least 45 minutes or more, depending on the size of your squash.
4. Allow to cool to room temperature before slicing open and removing the seedy stuff.
5. Spoon meat away from the tough outer skin and place into blender.
6. Wash cherries and add to squash along with flaxseeds.
7. Purée until nice and smooth.

Incredible Spinach Zucchini (6+)

This purée is fabulous for getting loads of veggies into your baby—it might just be our healthiest one! (Probably the lowest in naturally-occurring sugars.)

INGREDIENTS:

½ small yam

½ medium zucchini

Olive oil

Sea salt and peper to taste

¼ cup chopped fresh spinach

METHOD:

1. Preheat oven to 350°F.
2. Cut yam and zucchini into one-inch chunks and place in baking dish.
3. Drizzle with olive oil, season with salt and pepper, and roast in oven until tender, about 35 minutes.
4. Remove from oven and allow to cool.
5. Place cooked veggies and raw spinach into the blender and purée until even and smooth. Thin with breastmilk or unsweetened coconut milk if needed.

Simply Avocado and Banana (6+)

This super-simple purée is always a hit—it's mellow and very creamy in texture.

INGREDIENTS:

1 avocado

1 banana

METHOD:

1. Slice avocado lengthwise and remove pit.
2. Scoop out all that green goodness and throw it in the blender.
3. Peel banana and add to blender, then whip until mixture looks buttery.

Breezy Mornings Overnight Oats (6+)

Mornings just got easier. BAM! You have zero mess and a nutritious breakfast for the entire family, including your beautiful baby. These oats are a great addition to any of the purées from this section as well. Just grab a little of this and a little of that, and mix it up before you serve. You'll feel like a wizard.

TIP: Be mindful when introducing your baby to new foods, especially potential allergens like nuts and honey. For this reason, we recommend using non-nut milks (like coconut) and alternative natural sweeteners (like pure maple syrup) until your baby is about 12 months old. This recipe makes 4 full mason jars' worth.

INGREDIENTS:

4 cups gluten-free rolled oats

2 tsp . cinnamon or pumpkin pie spice

½ tsp . sea salt

4 tbsp . pure maple syrup

1 tsp . pure vanilla extract

4 cups unsweetened coconut milk

2 cups fresh fruit, chopped into small, baby-size bites

Sprinkle of flaxseeds

Coconut milk or soy yogurt

Sprinkle of chia seeds

Sprinkle of hemp hearts

METHOD:

1. Measure all of the dry ingredients evenly into mason jars.
2. Then, measure all of the wet ingredients (except fruit) evenly into the jars and seal.
3. Shake, shake, shake . . .
4. Open jars and top with chopped fresh fruit and a sprinkle of flaxseeds.
5. Re-seal the jars and pop into the fridge overnight or long enough that the liquids are absorbed and the oats are soft.
6. In the morning, open jars add a dollop of blueberry coconut milk yogurt or soy yogurt, and sprinkle with chia seeds and hemp hearts.

Mighty Mango (6+)

Mango is one of those rad purées that we always had in freezer bags stuffed with frozen cubes on hand at all times. On the days your baby turns her nose up at her dinner, you can add a cube of mango to it, and voila! The sweetness will make most things palatable enough that she'll eat it all.

INGREDIENTS:

One ripe mango

METHOD:

1. Remove peel from mango and cut around the pit as closely as possible to avoid waste.
2. Cut mango into chunks and simmer on stove until warmed, about 10 minutes.
3. Remove from heat, allowing to cool to room temperature before blending.
4. Once cool, blend until silky smooth.

Gas Attack

There are a handful of common foods that are really great for us nutritionally but are known contributors to gas and bloating. (Two things that you definitely want to avoid if you have a baby with a lot of tummy aches.) The following foods fall into this category:

- Beans
- Bell peppers
- Broccoli
- Brussels sprouts
- Cabbage
- Citrus
- Eggplant
- Tomatoes

Breakfast

Babies are usually pretty darn happy in the morning. The phrase "just happy to be here" describes this phenomenon perfectly. Because of this misunderstood happiness (who can possibly be that excited when they're packing two pounds of morning poop?!), they're also typically more open to trying new flavors and foods at this time.

Here's the secret to a successful breakfast: the meal needs to be nutritious, quick and simple to make and/or assemble, and be fit for the whole family. Why? Because we don't know about you, but we're zombies in the morning. Sure, we'll fake being alive and full of sunshine and rainbows and lollipops, but the truth is, all we want is an enormous cup of coffee and a second to gather ourselves. Do we get this when babies are involved? No. But life is easier when breakfast is easier because morning will be easier. And who wants a tough morning? No one. See below for gloriously simple, nutritious, delicious breakfast ideas.

You're welcome.

Spring Smoothie Bowl (6+)

This yummy breakfast is always a hit—with everyone. Repeat: you do not need to be a baby to love this nosh.

INGREDIENTS:

1 cup frozen peaches

1 slice watermelon

¼ cup coconut milk

1 tsp. hemp hearts

1 tsp. chia seeds

METHOD:

1. Place peaches, watermelon, and half the coconut milk in high-powered blender.
2. Begin to blend, slowly turning the power dial up from low to high. (The idea is for the concoction to be thick enough to eat with a spoon. However, if the mixture meets with too much resistance, add the rest of the coconut milk.)
3. Once mixture is fully blended into a thick, textured purée, stop blending and scoop into bowl.
4. Stir in hemp hearts and chia seeds and share this springtime breakfast with your baby.

Granola, 2 Ways (9+)

Because one version isn't enough.

GOJI GRANOLA

See recipe below and modify by adding 1 cup dried goji berries and 7 dried apple rings (cut into small pieces) before baking.

RAD BANANA GRANOLA

See recipe below and add 1 cup dried banana chips (crushed or chopped) and ½ cup raisins before baking.

INGREDIENTS:

3 cups rolled oats

½ cup pure maple syrup

¼ cup extra virgin olive oil

5 tbsp. chia seeds

Pinch of sea salt

METHOD:

1. Preheat oven to 225°F.
2. Combine all ingredients into large mixing bowl and stir until well combined.
3. Line a baking sheet with parchment paper and cover with moist granola mix.
4. Dust with cinnamon and bake for 25 minutes, checking and moving granola around with a spatula every 7-10 minutes. An easy way to check if your granola is ready for noshing: take a spoonful out of the oven and allow to cool to room temperature. If there's a crunch, it's ready.
5. Remove from oven and allow to cool to room temperature. Can be stored in an airtight container for up to two weeks.

Green Eggs (and no ham) Frittata (9+)

This recipe isn't completely plant-based, but we both believe that fresh, free-range eggs have a place in nutritious cooking. This makes 4 frittatas, but Tanya's older kids call these breakfast muffins. They're perfectly appropriate for the entire family, so we usually double the recipe.

INGREDIENTS:

8 egg yolks

¼ cup kale, washed and finely chopped

2 finely chopped sun-dried tomatoes or fresh cherry tomatoes

¼ cup Swiss chard, washed and finely chopped

Sprinkle of salt and pepper

2 tbsp. Daiya cheese

METHOD:

1. Preheat oven to 350°F.
2. Whip together all ingredients with a fork.
3. Grease muffin tins with extra virgin olive oil and pour egg batter into muffin tins, filling to top.
4. Slide into oven and bake until no longer wet on top and a toothpick inserted into the center of the frittata comes out clean, roughly 25 minutes. Check every 5 minutes.
5. Remove from oven and allow to cool until just warm or room temperature.
6. Serve to your sweet little baby and the rest of your drooling family.

Banana Baby Cakes (9+)

This is a really basic, gluten-free, banana-based pancake that is high in both nutrients and deliciousness. (Keep these pancakes on the smaller side, so they're easier to flip—and baby-size!)

INGREDIENTS:

1 ripe banana, peeled

1 cup gluten-free oats

½ cup unsweetened coconut milk

1 tbsp. pure maple syrup

1 tsp. extra virgin olive oil

¼ tsp. baking soda

¼ tsp. baking powder

Dash cinnamon

Pinch salt

METHOD:

1. Combine all ingredients into blender and blend until smooth.
2. Pour onto skillet that has been sprayed with coconut oil and flip once golden.
3. Remove from heat, let cool until just warm, and serve.

Beets Me, Let's Eat . . . Oats! (9+)

This oatmeal is a super easy breakfast and can be made the night before, too! Simply make recipe, scoop into jars, and refrigerate overnight. In the morning, stir and serve! It's perfect for hot summer mornings, and kids love to eat weird stuff. (Like ours. Our weird kids love to eat weird stuff. Weird.)

INGREDIENTS:

1 cups gluten-free rolled oats

1 cup unsweetened coconut milk

6-8 fresh raspberries

2 tbsp. roasted beets, finely diced

1 tbsp. pure maple syrup

1 tbsp. chia seeds

1 tsp. hemp hearts

½ tsp. cinnamon

¼ tsp. pure vanilla extract

Pinch sea salt

2 tbsp. soy yogurt

METHOD:

1. Layer all ingredients—except for yogurt—into mason jar(s), and seal with lids.
2. Shake, shake, shake . . .
3. Store in refrigerator overnight or long enough that the liquids are absorbed and the oats are soft.
4. Prior to serving, stir in the yogurt.

Carrot Swirl Pancakes (9+)

This fun recipe is a twist on Banana Baby Cakes (page 114); it adds a colorful veggie swirl! (Keep these pancakes on the smaller side, so they're easier to flip—and baby-size!)

INGREDIENTS:

Banana Baby Cakes batter (see page 114)

1 carrot

1 tsp. fresh grated ginger

METHOD:

1. Wash and peel carrot and cut into sticks about 2 to 3 inches long.
2. Pop carrot pieces into steamer basket and steam until soft.
3. Place cooked carrot and fresh ginger in blender and purée until smooth.
4. Pour Banana Baby Cake batter onto skillet sprayed with coconut oil.
5. After pouring, but before you give the baby cake its first flip, spoon some carrot onto the cooking batter and swirl it around a bit, creating a marbled look.
6. Flip your pancake.
7. Once pancakes are done, allow to cool to just warm.
8. Serve swirl-side-up and top with some applesauce or Strawberry Chia Jam (see page 205).

Blueberry-Peach Tofu Whip (6+)

This delicious cup of wonder could easily be a dessert. It's super yummy and absolutely teeming with plant-based protein and fiber (which we love).

INGREDIENTS:

1 cup organic soft tofu

1 peach, pitted

½ cup blueberries

1 tsp. chia seeds

METHOD:

1. Place ingredients in food processor and process until smooth.
2. Place mixture in storage container with lid and refrigerate overnight.
3. In the morning, scrape into serving dish, stir, and serve!

Quick Quinoa (6+)

Who says oatmeal has to get all the hot cereal props?! Not us. Quinoa is a complete protein and makes for a fab breakfast food.

INGREDIENTS:

¼ ripe banana

½ cup cooked quinoa

¼ cup unsweetened coconut milk

Sprinkle of cinnamon

METHOD:

1. Mash the banana well.
2. Place in pot with quinoa and coconut milk.
3. Stir well while heating to warm.
4. Remove from heat and allow to cool to just slightly warm.
5. Sprinkle with cinnamon and serve!

TIP: While oats can sometimes contain traces of gluten if they're farmed close to wheat, quinoa is fully gluten-free. Technically a seed, quinoa hails from South America. Enjoy!

Oats à la Otis (9+)

Our oatmeal rule of thumb is simple: half the dry or double the wet. It almost always results in a nice, moist oatmeal—not as runny as gruel and not as stiff as your momma made it.

INGREDIENTS:

½ cup gluten-free steel-cut oats

1 cup unsweetened coconut or almond milk

1 tsp. cinnamon

1 tsp. chia seeds

1 tsp. flaxseeds

1 tsp. hemp hearts

¼ banana, minced

1 strawberry, minced

METHOD:

1. Grease a medium-size cooking pot with coconut oil and add the oats.
2. Toast the oats slightly on medium heat, moving constantly.
3. Add milk and cinnamon and bring to just a boil while stirring.
4. Reduce heat and continue to cook on low for another 10 minutes.
5. Stir in chia seeds, flaxseeds, and hemp hearts, and remove from heat, allowing to cool to lukewarm.
6. Top with diced fruit and serve with a spoon . . . or let your baby caveman it by scooping and chowing with her hands.

Popeye Pancakes (9+)

These suckers are green, which really impresses older children (and spouses). They will never taste the spinach, and you'll love knowing they just ate it for breakfast.

INGREDIENTS:

½ cup gluten-free rolled oats

1 free-range egg or 2 yolks

½ cup spinach

1 tsp. cinnamon

1 tbsp. pure maple syrup

1 tsp. baking powder

2 tsp. Blueberry Chia Jam (page 205) plus more for serving

METHOD:

1. Combine all ingredients in blender and purée until smooth.

2. Pour batter onto heated skillet that has been greased with coconut oil.

3. Once tops look bubbly and edges are starting to dry out slightly, flip.

4. When other side is done, remove from heat, allow to cool until just warm, and serve with Blueberry Chia Jam (page 205).

Sanity Saving TIP: make an extra large batch and throw the leftover (cooled) pancakes into a freezer bag. They're perfect for popping into the toaster for a nutritious and warm breakfast or snack when you're pressed for time!

Red Velvet Beet Pancakes (9+)

As with the Popeye Pancakes (see page 123), the color of these guys will impress your whole family. If you're into making a fancy breakfast on Christmas morning, the combination of these two types of pancakes will really do the trick.

INGREDIENTS:

½ cup gluten-free steel-cut oats

1 free-range egg or 2 yolks

¼ cup chopped cooked beet

1 tsp. cinnamon

1 tbsp. pure maple syrup

1 tsp. baking powder

1 tsp. coconut oil

METHOD:

1. Combine all ingredients in blender and purée until smooth.
2. Spoon batter onto hot griddle.
3. Once tops look bubbly and edges are starting to dry out slightly, flip.
4. When other side is done, remove from heat, allow to cool until just warm, and serve with fresh blackberries and pure maple syrup, or Strawberry Chia Jam (see page 205).

Sweet Potato Polka-Dot Patties (9+)

This recipe could technically be a breakfast, lunch, dinner, and fast food. These suckers are easy to make, store, reheat, and take with you anywhere. (And they are nutritious.)

INGREDIENTS:

2 sweet potatoes

1 banana

Sprinkle of cinnamon

Handful of green peas

METHOD:

1. Preheat oven to 350°F.
2. Slice sweet potatoes lengthwise, wrap in foil, and pop into the oven, baking until soft, about 20 minutes. (This step can be done the night before, while you're making supper, and then stored in the refrigerator until the next day.)
3. Scrape out the soft insides of the potato and spoon into blender with banana and a pinch of cinnamon.
4. Blend until semi-smooth. If it's too thick, you can add water or breastmilk, a little at a time, to thin.
5. Pour onto warm griddle and dot with green peas before flipping.
6. Cool before serving; these hold their shape best when at room temperature or chilled.
7. Serve with Blueberry Chia Jam (see page 205) or pure maple syrup.

Falling for Oat Apple Pancakes (9+)

These delicious pancakes will have you dreaming of cozy Fair Isle sweaters and walks in crunchy amber-colored leaves.

INGREDIENTS:

2 cups unsweetened coconut milk

1 cup gluten-free rolled oats

1 tsp. cinnamon

1 tsp. vanilla extract

Pinch of salt

1 apple, peeled, cored, and sliced into thin wedges

METHOD:

1. Combine all ingredients except apple and stir or whisk together until the oats thicken up slightly and everything is well combined. (For a smoother pancake, you can blend the ingredients.)
2. Grease cast-iron pan with coconut oil and ladle batter onto pan in medium-size pancakes.
3. As soon as batter is poured, top with sliced apple.
4. Flip, and continue to cook until golden on both sides.
5. Serve immediately, allowing to cool a tad before cutting and offering to your little one.
6. If you're feeling treatsy, drizzle with a touch of pure maple syrup or some Strawberry Chia Jam (see page 205).

Garden Omelet (9+)

These are great for the whole family, and babies as young as nine months can partake in the enjoyment. They're full of protein and veggies—who can complain?

INGREDIENTS:

2 free-range egg yolks

1 tbsp. shredded peeled carrot (we use a cheese grater)

1 tbsp. finely chopped spinach

Pinch of salt and pepper

1 tbsp. Daiya cheese

METHOD:

1. Grease skillet with extra virgin olive oil and let it warm up.
2. Combine all ingredients except Daiya into bowl and whip with a fork.
3. Pour onto warm pan and cook until top begins to set up slightly.
4. Flip egg and cover one half with shredded Daiya cheese.
5. Fold cooked egg in half—plain side on top of cheesy side—and slide off skillet.
6. Allow to cool before cutting into bite-size pieces and serving.

Future Farmer Breakfast Scramble (12+)

This is a great way to use leftover corn on the cob and potatoes. Grandpa Dave would be so proud.

INGREDIENTS:

½ cob of GMO-free corn

1 free-range egg yolk

1 red potato, diced small

1 tsp. chives

2 tbsp. peas

¼ cup chopped fresh spinach

METHOD:

1. Remove corn from cob by taking a sharp knife and, holding the cob away from you, sliding it from the top to the bottom of the cob, carefully.
2. Combine all ingredients in cast-iron skillet with a drizzle of extra virgin olive oil.
3. Fry until eggs and potatoes are thoroughly cooked.
4. Allow to cool slightly before serving.

Whipped Raspberry Oatmeal (6+)

Honestly, this recipe looks too beautiful to eat (but then we do it, anyway). It's a hit for all ages, and your baby will love it as much as you will.

INGREDIENTS:

½ cup gluten-free rolled oats

1 cup coconut milk

1 tsp. cinnamon

1 tsp. vanilla extract

⅓ cup raspberries

1 tbsp. chia seeds

1 tbsp. hemp hearts

METHOD:

1. In a medium saucepan, combine oats, coconut milk, cinnamon, and vanilla.
2. Stirring constantly, bring to boil and reduce heat to medium-low.
3. Simmer for another 10 minutes until oatmeal starts to thicken up.
4. Remove from heat, allowing to cool slightly.
5. Pour oatmeal into blender along with raspberries and purée until it has a slightly whipped appearance.
6. Stir in chia seeds and hemp hearts.
7. Serve with a spoon—or in a squeeze pouch if you're on the go.

Lunch + Dinner

Lunch and dinner can be stressful if you're not prepared, which is why we definitely suggest getting into the habit of meal planning. Once a week, when you have a quiet thirty minutes or so (we actually laughed as we wrote that), prioritize creating a list of meals that you'll be making for the week. When you have it figured out, go grocery shopping for all of the ingredients you'll need, plus whatever else you're low on. This way, you won't have to think about what to make for dinner, what you may or may not have on hand in your fridge, or whether or not something will work for everyone.

You can lug your family to the beach, lazily stagger back to your home around five, and have the satisfaction of knowing what your family will eat ahead of time. You'll have already thought of this moment! Meal planning saves time and money and, most importantly, reduces stress.

Go, Me! Gomai (9+)

This yummy dish takes less than 5 minutes to make and is full of iron and protein. It makes enough for 2–4 baby-size servings, so if you're making it for the whole family, we recommend doubling it. (Don't worry—spinach shrinks. Like mushrooms . . . or your memory after having kids.)

INGREDIENTS:

1 bunch organic spinach

2 tbsp. water

2 tbsp. seed butter (like sunflower)

Pinch of sea salt (optional)

METHOD:

1. Wash, dry, and chop spinach into small pieces.
2. Place spinach and water in frying pan and sauté in water until spinach is just wilted (2–4 minutes).
3. Remove spinach from pan, drain excess water, and press remainder of water out by placing spinach between paper towels and patting firmly.
4. Place spinach in bowl and toss with seed butter until evenly distributed.
5. Sprinkle with sea salt (optional), and serve.

Curried Cauliflower + Chickpea Mash (9+)

Sometimes curry can cause your baby to produce more gas, so if you have a gassy baby already, you may want to leave the curry out.

TIP: For older noshers, try adding more veggies, such as whole peas, thin strips of green onion and carrot, and even finely diced beet!

INGREDIENTS:

½ cup water

½ cup vegetable broth (no added salt)

4 cups cauliflower florets

1 cup rehydrated (or canned) chickpeas

¼ tsp. mild curry powder

METHOD:

1. Bring water and broth to a boil.
2. Add cauliflower and chickpeas.
3. Mix, then cover with lid, and turn down to simmer for about 10 minutes.
4. Remove from heat, drain, and let cool until warm.
5. Place in blender with curry powder and blend until mostly smooth but still slightly chunky.
6. Serve, and save the extra for tomorrow's meal, too! This can also be frozen.

No-Cheese Cheesy Pasta (9+)

The sauce is great served over your favorite gluten-free pasta, rice, or cauli-flower steak.

INGREDIENTS:

1 cup gluten-free pasta

2 carrots, peeled and chopped into chunks

½ cup orange cauliflower (regular is fine, too)

Pinch of salt

Pinch of dried thyme

2 tbsp. Daiya cheese

METHOD:

1. Cook your pasta according to package directions and set aside.
2. Place carrots and cauliflower into medium saucepan and add water to just about covering (but not quite).
3. Bring to boil and reduce heat, cooking until veggies are tender. Remove from heat and place in blender. Add a pinch of salt and a pinch of thyme.
4. Blend until semi-smooth—but not too much. Small chunks are good.
5. Place back into saucepan, adding two tablespoons of Daiya cheese, and warm until melted.
6. Toss with pasta and enjoy.

Purple People-Eater Cauliflower Steaks (12+)

These suckers look seriously professional, and we promise you'll impress yourself. They're awesome eats for all ages, and they look super gourmet.

INGREDIENTS:

1 head purple cauliflower

1 tbsp. extra virgin olive oil *or* parchment paper

Sea salt to taste

1 clove garlic, pressed

METHOD:

1. Preheat oven to 325°F.
2. Remove leaves from head of cauliflower, leaving stem attached—this is important!
3. Cut two, 1-inch-thick slices down center of cauliflower, right into the stem. These are your steaks, so they should be flat on both sides.
4. Place steaks on baking sheet greased with olive oil or lined with parchment paper.
5. Drizzle with oil, sprinkle with sea salt and garlic.
6. Bake on center rack for 20 minutes, flip, then bake another 10 minutes or until cauliflower is tender.
7. Serve plain or with one of our vegan cheese sauces (see pages 207).

Coconut-Bean Stew (9+)

Once your baby is a little older, you can begin adding more vegetables (like roots and squash) to this recipe. The result is a chunkier, more filling stew.

INGREDIENTS:

1 tbsp. coconut oil

¼ cup finely chopped white onion

1 tsp. cumin

½ tsp. ground coriander

½ tsp. turmeric

2½ cups vegetable broth

1 cup dried red lentils, rinsed

Sea salt to taste (optional)

METHOD:

1. Heat coconut oil in medium-size pot, and sauté onion for 5 minutes until soft.
2. Add spices and cook for 2 more minutes.
3. Add broth to pot and turn heat up to a boil.
4. Add rinsed lentils and turn heat down to simmer.
5. Partially cover and cook for about 20 minutes.
6. Remove from heat, add sea salt (optional), and stir. Serve warm.

Honey-Dill-Glazed Carrot Bites (12+)

This is a fun twist on steamed carrots—and one that the whole family will love. The carrots will be soft enough for your little one and flavorful enough for your whole family.

INGREDIENTS:

1 carrot

1 tbsp. extra virgin olive oil

1 tbsp. honey

1 tsp. dill

1 orange

METHOD:

1. Wash and peel carrot, slicing into rounds, about ¼-inch-thick.
2. On medium heat, warm oil in cast-iron pan.
3. Add carrot, honey, and dill, giving a quick stir to coat.
4. Squeeze in the juice of one orange.
5. Reduce heat to low and continue to cook until carrot rounds are soft.
6. Cool to room temperature and serve.

Roasted Beets with Goat Cheese (9+)

Feta cheese works well with this recipe because it crumbles easily. Just make sure it's actually real feta—if it's made in North America, chances are it's from a cow (whose protein many people have a hard time digesting) and not a goat.

INGREDIENTS:

1 large beet

1 tbsp. soft goat cheese

METHOD:

1. Preheat oven to 350°F.
2. Without peeling (so many great nutrients are stored in a beet's peel!), slice ends off of beet, wrap in tin foil, and place in oven-safe dish in the pre-heated oven.
3. Roast for 45 minutes or until beet can be easily sliced with very little or no resistance. Remove from oven, remove foil, and allow to cool for about 15 minutes.
4. Once the beet is cool enough to handle, simply slice beet into small pieces and top with crumbled goat cheese.

Look at you! You're practically gourmet.

Jack and the Masala-Glazed Beanstalk (12+)

If your baby is younger than 12 months, these beans are also very tasty puréed.

INGREDIENTS:

1 cup fresh green beans (any color will do)

1 tsp. extra virgin olive oil

½ tsp. masala spice

Pinch of sea salt

1 tsp. nutritional yeast

2 tbsp. water

METHOD:

1. Wash beans and cut the tips off both ends.
2. In a heated cast-iron pan, warm olive oil.
3. Add beans, masala spice, salt, and nutritional yeast.
4. Sauté briefly.
5. Add 2 tablespoons of water and cover for 5 minutes, just long enough for the beans to soften up.
6. Cool before serving to your baby.

Battered Banana Bites (12+)

You can use any of our pancake recipes to batter these 'nanners. Our favorite is the Popeye Pancake, which will give these suckers an extra shot of veggies and color.

INGREDIENTS:

1 banana, peeled

Popeye Pancake batter (see page 123)

METHOD:

1. Grease pan with coconut oil and warm.
2. Slice banana into rounds, half an inch thick.
3. Dip banana pieces into batter and fry until golden on each side.
4. Allow to cool before serving with pure maple syrup, chia jam, or seed butter.

Cheesy Pasta with Strawberries and Shredded Kale (12+)

Serve this one to your baby, sans spoon. This dish is great for texture, color, and flavor exploration. Let those chubby little hands get messy!

INGREDIENTS:

1 cup gluten-free pasta of your choice

1 tsp. extra virgin olive oil

1 tbsp. nutritional yeast

2 fresh strawberries, sliced into bite-size pieces

¼ cup finely chopped raw kale

METHOD:

1. Cook pasta according to package specifications.
2. Drain excess water from pasta.
3. Drizzle up to a teaspoon of oil over pasta and sprinkle nutritional yeast. Toss.
4. Add prepared strawberries and kale and toss again.
5. Serve immediately.

Not Yo' Momma's Creamy Veggie Pasta (12+)

This dish is seriously yummy, and its components are small enough that your baby can go to town without worry. Great for all ages.

INGREDIENTS:

1 cup gluten-free pasta, or quinoa

½ cup raw cauliflower, washed and chopped

¼ cup fresh spinach

1 tsp. extra virgin olive oil

3 tbsp. Daiya cheese

Salt and pepper to taste

METHOD:

1. Cook pasta or quinoa to package specifications, drain if necessary, and set aside.
2. In a medium saucepan, steam the fresh cauliflower until it is just starting to get soft.
3. Combine the warm, cooked cauliflower, spinach, olive oil, Daiya cheese, and a pinch of salt and pepper in blender.
4. Purée until smooth (the warmth from the cauliflower will melt the cheese).
5. Pour sauce over pasta or quinoa and serve.

Coconut Zoodles (9+)

These "noodles" are delicious served just as they are, but they are extra delicious under one of our super fantastic sauces!

INGREDIENTS:

1 small zucchini

1 tbsp. coconut oil

METHOD:

1. Wash and peel zucchini.
2. Using a spiralizer (or for those us who do things the more rustic way, a grater), shave zucchini so it resemble noodles.
3. Warm coconut oil in a cast-iron pan and sauté zoodles on medium heat for 5 minutes, stirring constantly.
4. Remove from heat, let cool to just warm, and serve plain—or top with a little nutritional yeast.

The Making of a BRAT

If ever there was a tried-and-true method of stopping diarrhea, it was the BRAT diet. An acronym for bananas, rice, applesauce, and toast, this diet will quickly absorb extra water and create bulk in the intestine to stop loose stool. In a child over the age of nine months, this preparation can be a godsend when faced with this fairly common childhood affliction.

For added nutrients, be sure to use gluten-free (if your baby's sensitive) or whole grain bread and sprouted brown rice. Feed these four foods to your child throughout the day (with plenty of water, as you would with anyone suffering from diarrhea—you don't want your baby to become dehydrated), and you'll develop a brand new appreciation for the combination of these simple yet effective foods.

Smoothies + Juices

Aside from water (which should be your baby's primary source of hydration after twelve months) and milk alternatives (from which your baby will still get most of her nourishment until about nine months old), how do you hydrate your baby without inadvertently hooking her up with a shot of processed sugar?

The answer is fresh-pressed juices and smoothies.

Fresh-pressed juice is juice that is extracted directly from fruits and vegetables and contains no added *anything*. It's super hydrating and chock-full of micronutrients, such as vitamins and antioxidants.

For a heavier snack or meal supplement, smoothies are our go-to. They contain whole fruits and veggies, which includes fiber. They're filling, and when your baby becomes obsessed with drinking out of a straw (circa 12 months old), she'll love herself a li'l smoothie.

Pretty in Pink Juice (9+)

Our definition of a "watermelon slice," is one full round slice of a whole watermelon. (FYI)

INGREDIENTS:

6 strawberries

Handful of raspberries

1 watermelon slice

METHOD:

1. Juice ingredients in order they are given.
2. Give to your baby to drink immediately! (Add some ice if you want to keep it cooler for longer, and shake every few minutes as your baby is drinking to avoid separation.)

Sunshine Juice (6+)

This juice is inherently sweet, so if offering to a baby under the age of one year, we recommend diluting with filtered water. (A half-to-half ratio is good.)

INGREDIENTS:

2 carrots

1 orange, peeled

2 pineapple spears

METHOD:

1. Run the ingredients through your juicer in the order given.
2. Give to your baby to drink immediately! (Add some ice if you want to keep it cooler for longer, and shake every few minutes as your baby drinks it to avoid separation.)

Almond-Date Smoothie with Strawberry (12+)

If you're nervous about using almond milk (maybe your baby hasn't been introduced to any nut products yet?), swap for unsweetened coconut milk instead. Also, don't think more is better when it comes to dates—they might be crazy high in fiber, but they're also very sweet. (And make sure that those dates are truly pit-free. Safety first, ladies and gents!)

INGREDIENTS:

1 cup unsweetened almond milk

1 banana

1 cup strawberries

3 pitted dates

METHOD:

1. Place all ingredients together in high-powered blender and blend until smooth.
2. Serve immediately.

TIP: This is the perfect smoothie to share with your baby because this recipe makes about 3 cups' worth!

Green Goodness Smoothie (9+)

We fed this smoothie to Otis and Ariya while photographing it, then Ariya's parents drank some, and then we greedily slurped up the rest. It's a delicious and nutritious all-ages kinda drink.

INGREDIENTS:

1 banana
1 cup green grapes
1 kale leaf
1 cup frozen pineapple
6 fresh mint leaves
1 cup water
1 tsp. hemp hearts (optional)
1 tsp. chia seeds (optional)

METHOD:

1. Combine all ingredients—except hemp hearts and chia seeds—in a blender, and blend until smooth.
2. Sprinkle with hemp hearts and chia seeds for extra awesomeness.

Hulk Smoothie (9+)

This smoothie is great for babies because iron is more readily absorbed when accompanied by vitamin C. This is where the true beauty of this smoothie lies— it's very high in iron, vitamin C, and protein.

INGREDIENTS:

1 cup fresh spinach, washed

½ orange, peeled

8 frozen strawberries

½ cup coconut milk or water

1 tbsp. hemp hearts

METHOD:

Combine all ingredients in blender and blend until smooth. If your baby is funny about the texture of the hemp hearts, then just leave them out.

Color Me Kale (9+)

This recipe makes a large smoothie; perfect for sharing with other siblings or sleep-deprived parents in desperate need of a jolt of energy and goodness.

INGREDIENTS:

½ cup chopped, fresh kale

1 cup frozen mango chunks

½ cup frozen strawberries

(Up to) 1 cup water

1 tbsp. shredded or shaved coconut

1 tsp. chia seeds

METHOD:

1. Combine first 4 ingredients in blender and purée until smooth, adding the water slowly to thin. (Don't add too much, though—this smoothie is tastiest when it's on the thick side.)
2. Sprinkle with shredded or shaved coconut and chia seeds before serving.

Strawberry Rhubarb Smoothie (12+)

This smoothie is best for babies twelve months and older due to the acidity of the rhubarb. But if your baby is handling citrus without any problems, she may be fine sipping this treat sooner.

INGREDIENTS:

¾ cup fresh strawberries

¼ cup frozen chopped rhubarb

¼ cup vanilla coconut yogurt

¼ cup water

METHOD:

1. Combine all ingredients in blender and purée, adding water a little bit at a time to thin if necessary.
2. Sip, sip, sip.

Food on the Run

Because babies have fast metabolisms and constantly require fuel, they eat ALL. THE. TIME. Because you have a busy life and have other stuff to do aside from eating, sleeping, and pooping, you need to arm yourself with great snack ideas that you can easily tote around with you while you get from your older daughter's dance recital to your son's soccer game. Or to the grocery store. Or to work.

Or to the liquor store. Just kidding. (Sort of.)

We've come up with a few goodies that travel well, are highly nutritive, and are extremely baby- *and* mommy-friendly alike. So go ahead—leave your house! You know you want to.

Assorted Date Balls (12+)

These little snacks are packed full of fiber, protein, and good carbs. They're very easy to make and even simpler to transport. If your little one doesn't like coconut, feel free to roll the balls in something else, like sesame seeds. Or nothing at all—it's up to you! Make these your own creation.

INGREDIENTS:

2 cups pitted dates

¾ cup gluten-free rolled oats

½ cup warm water

¼ cup sesame seeds

¼ cup hemp hearts

¼ cup dried cranberries

1 tbsp. chia seeds

½ cup unsweetened shredded coconut

METHOD:

1. Mix all ingredients except coconut together in food processor until well combined.
2. Roll into small balls, dip in coconut, and place in mini muffin liners as you go.
3. Stack mini muffin liners in an airtight container and store in the refrigerator for up to 2 weeks.

Rainbow Fruit Kabobs (12+)

Melon and pineapple work especially well for this. If your baby loves dipping things (of course she loves dipping things!), you can offer Zesty Yogurt Dip (see page 213).

INGREDIENTS:

4 bite-size pieces of watermelon

4 bite-size pieces of honeydew

4 bite-size pieces of pineapple

2 kiwis, sliced into quarters

4 strawberries, sliced into quarters

4 firm (good quality) straws

METHOD:

1. Pierce fruit with straws, assemble in any order you'd like!
2. Pack to bring on a trip, or serve right then and there at home.
3. Provide dip if desired.

TIP: For a cute variation, you can use cookie cutters to make shapes with the fruit, instead of sliding on sticks or straws.

Chewy Nut-Free Granola Bars (12+)

For soft and chewy bars, keep at room temperature. For harder bars, store in the fridge. The refrigerated bars are great for teething toddlers, because they are cool and your baby can get her gnaw on. This recipe makes 16 bars.

INGREDIENTS:

2½ cups gluten-free rolled oats
¼ cup roasted pumpkin seeds, chopped
¼ cup roasted sunflower seeds, chopped
¼ cup unsalted butter (or soft-solid coconut oil), cut into pieces
⅓ cup honey
¼ cup brown coconut sugar
½ tsp. vanilla extract
1 tbsp. seed butter
¼ tsp. salt
½ cup raisins, coarsely chopped
¼ cup dates, pitted and chopped
3 tbsp. hemp hearts
2 tbsp. chia seeds
4 tbsp. shredded unsweetened coconut

METHOD:

1. In a large, ungreased frying pan, toast oats and seeds over medium heat for about 5 minutes.
2. Transfer to large mixing bowl.
3. Combine butter (or coconut oil), honey, brown coconut sugar, vanilla extract, seed butter, and the salt in a small saucepan over medium heat.
4. Cook, stirring occasionally, until solids melt, and the sugar completely dissolves.
5. Pour butter mixture into bowl with raisins, dates, and the toasted oats and seeds. Mix well.
6. Let cool 5 minutes then add hemp hearts, chia seeds, and coconut. Stir to combine.
7. Transfer oat mixture to 9"x9" pan greased with coconut oil or lined with parchment paper. Use damp finger tips to firmly press the mixture into the pan. (Press hard here, so the bars will stay together once cooled and cut.)
8. Cover, then refrigerate at least 2 hours.
9. Cut into two rows of 8 bars, making 16 in total.
10. Store bars in an airtight container in the refrigerator for up to one week.

Roasted Chickpeas, 2 Ways (12+)

Roasted chickpeas are a great way to get fiber and protein into your baby while offering a fun, pint-size snack. These suckers are super addictive and are a great replacement for chips or conventional popcorn for your older children, too.

SAVORY ROASTED CHICKPEAS

INGREDIENTS:

½ cup rehydrated chickpeas

1 tbsp. olive oil

1 clove garlic, pressed

Pinch salt

METHOD:

1. Preheat oven to 350°F.
2. Toss all ingredients in bowl and pour onto parchment-lined baking sheet.
3. Bake for 30 minutes, moving chickpeas every 10 minutes.
4. Allow to cool before serving.

SWEET ROASTED CHICKPEAS

INGREDIENTS:

½ cup rehydrated chick peas

1 tbsp. pure maple syrup

Sprinkle of cinnamon

METHOD:

1. Preheat oven to 350°F.
2. Toss all ingredients in bowl and pour onto parchment-lined baking sheet.
3. Bake for 30 minutes, moving chickpeas every 10 minutes.
4. Allow to cool before serving.

Kind Kale Chips (12+)

Green kale is just fine, but purple kale makes these chips pretty and colorful—
two of baby's favorite things to put in her mouth!

INGREDIENTS:

1 small bunch of kale

1 tbsp. extra virgin olive oil

1 tsp. nutritional yeast

¼ tsp. sea salt

METHOD:

1. Preheat oven to 350°F.
2. Wash and dry kale, then chop into bite-size pieces.
3. Place in a bowl, add oil, and massage the kale until evenly coated.
4. Spread out kale evenly on baking sheet in a single layer.
5. Bake for 6–10 minutes, keeping an eye on it—it will burn quickly.
6. Remove from oven when edges become crisp and begin to lightly brown.
7. Sprinkle with salt and yeast and either serve immediately (making sure they're not too hot), or let cool completely and store up to 4 hours in a glass container lined with a paper towel to absorb excess moisture.

Pineapple Banana Bakes (9+)

These dense, gluten-free muffins are perfect for bringing with you wherever the day may take you. They are high in protein (lots of oats!) and taste alike.

INGREDIENTS:

1½ cups gluten-free rolled oats

Dash cinnamon

½ tsp. orange zest

Pinch salt

1⅓ cups unsweetened coconut milk

½ banana, chopped

½ cup chopped fresh pineapple

1 tbsp. pure maple syrup

METHOD:

1. Preheat oven to 350°F.
2. Combine oats, cinnamon, zest, salt, and milk in blender.
3. Blend on low for about 20 seconds (you want the oats to remain coarse).
4. Add banana, pineapple, and maple syrup, and stir.
5. Spoon into lined or greased muffin tins, filling to top.
6. Sprinkle tops with cinnamon.
7. Bake for 25 minutes. (Don't stress—these suckers don't rise.)
8. Cool completely before serving.

Yam Medallions (9+)

These yummy finger foods are great for babies and small children. They are soft enough for babies to handle and perfect to pack in preschool lunches, too.

INGREDIENTS:

2 yams

1 tbsp. extra virgin olive oil

Sea salt to taste

METHOD:

1. Preheat oven at 325°F.
2. Peel and slice two yams into thin circles using cheese grater or mandoline.
3. Place in bowl and massage pieces with oil.
4. Spread oiled pieces across baking sheet lined with parchment paper. The yams can touch but shouldn't overlap.
5. Sprinkle with minimal sea salt.
6. Place baking sheet in oven, and bake for 30 minutes or until edges are just starting to dry out. (Check the yams every 10 minutes to ensure they don't overcook. You want them crispy but not hard.)
7. Remove from oven and spread out on cutting board, allowing to cool. They will get crispier once cooled.

Enjoy with your bambino!

Yam Chips (12+)

As opposed to Yam Medallions (see page 193), these chips are thinner and therefore crunchier, which is why we recommend them for babies who are over a year old.

INGREDIENTS:

1 large yam

1 tbsp. extra virgin olive oil

Sprinkle sea salt

METHOD:

1. Preheat oven to 325°F.
2. Wash, peel, and slice yam into very thin pieces using mandoline or the side of a cheese grater (the mandoline pieces will be far prettier).
3. In a bowl, massage pieces with olive oil.
4. Spread oiled pieces across baking sheet lined with parchment paper. The yams can touch but shouldn't overlap.
5. Sprinkle salt over top, sparingly.
6. Bake for 30 minutes or until edges are just starting to dry out.
7. While they're in the oven, check the yams every 10 minutes to ensure they don't overcook. You want them crispy but not hard.
8. Remove from the oven and spread out on a wooden cutting board, allowing them to cool. (The yam chips will get crispier once cooled.)

Banana Energy Balls (9+)

These little bites are so yummy, they could easily be a dessert. Full of fiber and protein, they're the perfect snack for kids of all ages (and are easily transportable).

INGREDIENTS:

2 bananas, mashed

1 tbsp. pure maple syrup

½ tsp. stevia or coconut crystals

2 tbsp. almond butter or SuperButter (nut-free)

1 tsp. shredded unsweetened coconut

4 tbsp. coconut flour

2 tbsp. chia seeds

METHOD:

1. Preheat oven to 325°F.
2. In medium bowl, combine all ingredients except the coconut flour and the chia seeds.
3. Add coconut flour, a tablespoon at a time, mixing well between each addition, until it has the consistency of a slightly dry batter and holds its shape when formed.
4. Sprinkle some chia seeds into a shallow dish (a plate works well).
5. Roll into balls, then roll in chia seeds.
6. Bake on a parchment-lined baking sheet until slightly golden, maybe 10 minutes, checking often.
7. Cool and serve, breaking into smaller pieces for younger bambinos. Store in airtight container on the counter for up to a week.

Oatmeal Banana Bakes with Blueberry Buttons (12+)

This recipe is awesome to make when you have leftover oatmeal. Waste not, want not, right?

INGREDIENTS:

1 cup cooked oatmeal

2 bananas

5 tbsp. unsweetened coconut milk

1 tbsp. pure maple syrup

1 tsp. aluminum-free baking powder

1 tsp. cinnamon

1 tsp. pure vanilla extract

1 cup blueberries

METHOD:

1. Preheat oven to 350°F.
2. Combine all ingredients (except blueberries) in blender and purée until it has a smooth and even consistency.
3. Pour into muffin tins, greased with coconut oil, until about ⅔ full.
4. Dot the tops of batter with blueberries.
5. Bake for 15–20 minutes or until a toothpick inserted into center of bakes comes out clean.
6. Allow to cool before popping out of pan with the help of a spatula.
7. Serve once fully cooled.

About the Five-Second Rule

In a word (or two): practice it. Unless your baby's food fell into feces or vomit, the five-second rule can actually be a good thing.

The bacteria that babies pick up in infancy and early childhood can have a major effect on how well they handle viruses and bacteria as an adult. Basically, you need to *build* a great immune system to have one, so a little dirty watermelon is not going to hurt your baby—in fact, it'll help her.

So don't feel guilty the next time you hastily wipe off a cracker that's just fallen under the stroller and give it back to your little angel. You're being a better caregiver than you know—you're giving your baby the gift of a healthy immune system, and there is *a lot* of science to back these words up.

Rant over. (Drops mic.)

Dips + Spreads

Life cannot be lived without sauce. Sauce rocks, and your baby deserves to know that. Here are some recipes for tasty, healthy concoctions that your baby will love to get messy with. And since your baby loves to feed you, we promise you'll love these recipes, too. (PS: We've just been there, done that—there are no hidden cameras in your kitchen. Plus, we don't have the energy to be that creepy. We're moms. Come *on*.)

Strawberry Chia Jam (6+)

We use very ripe organic strawberries for this recipe, so they're soft and juicy. If you use less-ripe berries, you might need to add a tablespoon or two of water, or cook the berries down for 15 minutes before mashing.

The chia seeds will absorb the extra moisture and thicken the jam, so it's spreadable. Plus, it's raw, so you get all the benefits of raw fruit plus those super rad chia seeds full of omegas. You can freeze the leftover jam between servings—if it lasts that long (which it won't).

INGREDIENTS:

3 cups strawberries

1 tbsp. pure maple syrup

6 tbsp. chia seeds

METHOD:

1. Remove leaves and stems, wash berries well, and place in blender.
2. Mix until smooth with small chunks. You can purée for a smoother jam, or mash with a fork for a more rustic jam.
3. Add the syrup and mix for another 30 seconds.
4. Add the chia seeds and stir well.
5. Let sit 5 minutes and stir again.
6. Pour jam into mason jar and refrigerate overnight.
7. Serve in the morning on pancakes.

TIP: Feel free to mix it up by using blueberries instead of strawberries—this jam is a fabulous way to use bruised or overripe fruit.

Vegan Cheese Sauce, 2 Ways (9+)

Cheese sauce is one of those staples that every family uses. This plant-based variation is dairy- and gluten-free, so it's awesome for people who live with food sensitivities. We offer two variations: nut-free and a little nutty.

NUT-FREE VEGAN CHEESE SAUCE

INGREDIENTS:

2 carrots, peeled and chopped into chunks

½ cup orange cauliflower (white is fine, too)

1 tbsp. extra virgin olive oil

1 tsp. thyme

Salt and pepper to taste

2 tbsp. Daiya cheese

METHOD:

1. Place carrots and cauliflower in steamer basket and steam until tender.
2. Remove from heat and place in blender along with olive oil, thyme, and a pinch of salt and pepper.
3. Blend until semi-smooth (small chunks are good).
4. Pour into medium saucepan and reheat on stovetop, adding Daiya cheese and stirring until melted.
5. Serve over pasta, zoodles, or cauliflower steak.

A LITTLE NUTTY VEGAN CHEESE SAUCE

INGREDIENTS:

1 cup plain cashews

¼ cup unsweetened almond milk

1 tbsp. nutritional yeast

½ tsp. sea salt

METHOD:

1. Place cashews in dish and cover with water. Let soak for 2–4 hours.
2. Drain water and place cashews in blender.
3. Add rest of ingredients and blend until smooth and thick. If too thick, thin with a little extra almond milk.
4. Scrape from blender and use for pasta, veggies, or even a sandwich spread.

Hummus, 2 Ways (6+)

Babies love to dip and get messy, and hummus is their perfect collaborator. It's super high in plant-based protein and fiber as well as delicious on just about anything. We offer two variations: one using chickpeas (traditional) and one using soybeans.

MELLOW YELLOW HUMMUS

INGREDIENTS:

1 cup rehydrated or canned chickpeas
1 clove garlic, minced
1 tbsp. extra virgin olive oil
½ tbsp. lemon juice
¼ tsp. sea salt
1 tsp. sesame seeds

METHOD:

1. Combine everything—except sesame seeds—in food processor, and process until smooth.
2. Remove, sprinkle with sesame seeds, and serve with steamed veggies or grainy crackers.

LEAN + GREEN HUMMUS

INGREDIENTS:

1 cup shelled soybeans (edamame)
¼ cup fresh basil
1 clove garlic, minced
1 tbsp. extra virgin olive oil
½ tbsp. lime juice
½ tsp. fresh ginger, grated
¼ tsp. sea salt

METHOD:

1. Combine everything in food processor and process until smooth.
2. Remove and serve with steamed veggies or grainy crackers.

Cauliflower Alfredo Sauce (6+)

Again, life cannot be fully lived without a creamy alfredo sauce. Luckily, we've found a plant-based version that is both dairy-free and inherently nutritious. You're welcome.

INGREDIENTS:

1 small head organic cauliflower

1 clove garlic

2 tbsp. extra virgin olive oil

¼ cup unsweetened coconut milk

Salt and pepper

METHOD:

1. Preheat oven to 350°F.
2. Clean cauliflower and remove leaves and stem.
3. Sprinkle with 1 tbsp. olive oil and minced garlic.
4. Place on lined or greased baking sheet and bake until tender, around 30 minutes.
5. Remove from oven and place cauliflower in blender.
6. Blend on low, while adding coconut milk and remaining tablespoon of olive oil, a little at a time, until smooth and at desired consistency. (You may need to adjust the amount of milk depending on the size of your cauliflower.)
7. Add a pinch of salt and pepper to mixture and serve on spaghetti squash, cauliflower steaks, or zoodles.

Raw(ish) Asparagus-Spinach Pesto (9+)

This pesto is full of green goodness: it uses asparagus, spinach, and basil. We hope you fall in love.

INGREDIENTS:

1 small bunch asparagus

1 small bunch spinach

4 basil leaves

1 garlic clove, minced

⅓ cup water

1 tsp. lemon juice

Salt and pepper to taste

METHOD:

1. Wash asparagus, spinach, and basil.
2. Steam asparagus for a few minutes until bright green.
3. Combine all ingredients in food processor and process until relatively smooth.
4. Serve over rice or zoodles.

Zesty Yogurt Dip (6+)

This super simple recipe tastes fantastic when paired with fruit. (Any fruit.) If it's too tart for your baby, you can substitute the plain yogurt for a vanilla or fruit-flavored version.

INGREDIENTS:

Zest from ½ lemon, lime, or orange

½ cup plain soy yogurt

METHOD:

1. Wash fruit peel well and zest half.
2. Stir into soy yogurt and serve!

Hippie Harvest Sauce (9+)

This sauce is fantastic on gluten-free pasta, shredded squash, quinoa, and just about anything else you can think of. It's a must-try, folks.

INGREDIENTS:

1 tomato

1 red pepper

3 tbsp. extra virgin olive oil

1 tsp. white wine vinegar

½ white onion, diced

1 cup fresh spinach, chopped

Pinch of thyme

Salt and pepper to taste

METHOD:

1. Preheat oven to 375°F.
2. Cut tomato and pepper in half and remove pepper seeds and stem.
3. Place on baking sheet lined with parchment paper and place in oven.
4. Roast until peppers are soft and tomatoes appear blistered (about 25 minutes).
5. Meanwhile, combine 1 tbsp. of the oil, vinegar, onion, and spinach in pan on the stove.
6. Sauté mixture over medium heat until onion is soft. Set aside.
7. Remove veggies from oven and place in blender. Add sautéed onions and spinach. Blend on low until smooth.
8. Season with a pinch of thyme and salt and pepper to taste.
9. Serve on top of yellow summer squash noodles with lentil balls or chickpeas.

The Nitty Gritty on Choking

Every parent fears that their baby or child might choke on food, but there are some great ways to prevent this scary event from happening. Although not guaranteed, these ideas might help:

- Never leave your child alone while eating.

- Be diligent about slicing firmer finger foods into halves or even quarters. (A good rule of thumb is pea-size.)

- Know which foods are commonly choked on. These include (but aren't limited to): whole grapes, hard candy, hot dogs, popcorn, and whole nuts.

- Make sure you (and all caregivers) know how to give the Heimlich maneuver to infants and toddlers (it's *not* the same as the method used on older kids and adults). Taking a first aid class that teaches this can instill you with confidence.

Sweet Somethings

There is absolutely no way we could ever write any sort of recipe book without a dessert section. Sweet food is a must, and the recipes here use only unrefined, minimally processed, very natural sweeteners. (Like, mostly fruit.) And we'd be remiss to not offer a gluten-free birthday cake recipe, so we absolutely included one! We hope you and your little one(s) enjoy. xo

Pavlova Birthday Cake (12+)

This baby food cookbook wouldn't be very good without a recipe for a kick-ass first birthday cake. Pavlova is a bit of a labor of love because it's a two-part process. Because one of the steps entails leaving the oven door cracked while the pavlova cools after baking, we recommend actually making it right before bed and leaving the oven cracked overnight. This way, you're guaranteed to have a perfectly cooled and set pavlova, and nobody gets burned by an open oven door, which can be a safety issue with small children.

Happy birthday to you . . .

INGREDIENTS:

½ cup egg whites, at room temperature (from about 4 eggs)

⅛ tsp. cream of tartar

⅛ tsp. salt

1 cup granulated sugar

1½ tsp. cornstarch

½ tsp. pure vanilla extract

1¼ cups full-fat coconut milk

1 cup sliced strawberries

½ cup blueberries

Pieces of candied ginger (optional)

METHOD:

1. Preheat oven to 350°F.
2. Using an electric mixer, whip the egg whites, cream of tartar, and salt in a dry bowl until frothy.
3. Add the sugar, cornstarch, and vanilla, and continue whipping until stiff, smooth, and glossy. (About 10 minutes.)
4. On a sheet of parchment paper, use a pencil to draw or trace a circle that's 9 inches in diameter. (About the size of a round cake pan—this is what we use to trace our size guide.)

5. Line a baking sheet with the parchment circle, pencil side-down (you'll be able to see the circle through the paper).
6. Spoon egg white mixture onto the sheet, staying within your circle. Use the back of the spoon to smooth the top and sides.
7. Bake in the center of the oven for 10 minutes, then reduce heat to 300°F and bake until the meringue has puffed up and cracked on the top, or about 45 minutes. (The surface should be the color of a light Starbucks latte.)
8. Turn off the oven, open the door a crack, and let the pavlova cool to room temperature in the oven for at least 30 minutes. This ensures a gradual cooling, which protects the delicate meringue.
9. While cake is cooling, make your dairy-free coconut whip, adding honey or pure maple syrup to sweeten. (See page 237, and follow steps 1 through 5.)
10. Once cake is fully cooled, spoon whip onto the top of the meringue, and then decorate with fresh fruit and ginger.
11. Using a bread knife, slice into wedges before serving.

TIP: Because you have little ones running around your home, we recommend that you bake your pavlova at night, after your monkeys have gone to bed. This way, you can allow the meringue to cool properly, without worrying about little hands touching your hot, open oven.

Chia Pudding, 2 Ways (6+)

Both of these recipes can be thinned out with additional milk alternative or water and added to purées, such as blueberry.

COCONUT CHIA PUDDING

INGREDIENTS:

1 cup unsweetened coconut milk

4 tbsp. chia seeds

Sprinkle of cinnamon

METHOD:

1. Combine milk, seeds, and cinnamon in a glass jar, and stir very well.
2. Let sit on your counter for 5 minutes.
3. Stir again very well (should be thickening up), cover, and pop in the fridge overnight to set.
4. Serve cold.

FRUITY CHIA PUDDING

This version of chia pudding is the perfect baby food for brain power! As your wee one gets older, you can make this a bit less runny by cutting back the water. This fruity chia pudding is also great for squeeze pouches.

INGREDIENTS:

½ cup fruit (any kind—we like pears, blueberry, or even avocado)

1½ cups water

½ cup chia seeds

METHOD:

1. Combine fruit with water in blender and blend until smooth.
2. Pour into glass container. Add chia seeds, stir, and let sit on your counter for 5 minutes.
3. Stir again, cover, and place in the fridge overnight.
4. Serve cold.

Frozen Banana Whip with Shredded Coconut (6+)

This dessert has the consistency of smooth, creamy ice cream—sans dairy and added sugar. To get the desired result, a high-powered blender is a must; it won't be the same if you're using a regular one.

INGREDIENTS:

2 bananas, chopped and frozen

¼ cup unsweetened coconut milk

1 tsp. shredded or flaked coconut to garnish

METHOD:

1. Combine frozen bananas and milk in Vitamix or other high-powered blender.
2. Blend on high until it has an the consistency of ice cream.
3. Remove from blender, place in serving dish, and top with coconut.
4. Serve immediately!

Strawberry Almond Fruit Pops (9+)

Delicious and layered, your kids will be über impressed with your freezer skills.

INGREDIENTS:

1 cup fresh strawberries, tops removed

½ cup unsweetened almond milk

1 tbsp. pure maple syrup

METHOD:

1. Purée the strawberries and pour into popsicle molds until about ⅓ of the way full; set aside remaining purée in the fridge.
2. Pop ⅓-full molds into freezer and leave until firm.
3. Combine almond milk and syrup.
4. Pour milky mixture into the frozen molds, filling up to ⅔ full. Don't add too much or you won't be able to put your stick in at the end!
5. Place popsicles back in freezer until firm.
6. Top off the popsicle molds with remaining strawberry purée and insert your sticks.
7. Place the treats back in the freezer (last time, we promise!) until hard.
8. To remove, run a little hot water over the plastic molds to release ice pops.

Fall Fruit Compote (9+)

When we make this dessert for adults, we leave the peels on. But for babies, peels can present a possible choking hazard. We recommend you peel your fruit and let your compost eat the peels instead. You can vary this recipe for spring or summer fruits by simply substituting the apples and pears for berries and peaches. Enjoy!

INGREDIENTS:

4 apples, peeled and sliced

4 pears, peeled and sliced

½ cup pure maple syrup

¼ cup coconut oil

2 cups gluten-free rolled oats

1 tbsp. cinnamon

METHOD:

1. Preheat oven to 350°F.
2. Combine peeled and sliced fruit with maple syrup, mixing well.
3. Using 1 tbsp. of the coconut oil, grease a 9"x12" baking pan.
4. Pour fruit mixture in and spread around evenly.
5. Combine oats with cinnamon, mix, and pour over the fruit, distributing evenly.
6. Using the rest of the coconut oil, dab pea-size bits here and there around the top of the oats until it's used up.
7. Cover with foil and bake for 40 minutes.
8. Remove cover and bake for another 15 minutes.
9. Remove from oven and let cool until it's a good temperature for your baby.
10. Serve immediately or refrigerate and serve cold or at room temperature. Will keep in the fridge for up to a week.

TIP: This recipe makes enough for the whole family, but make no mistake—we can both pound it back all by ourselves. (Like, if there was such a thing as a compote-eating contest, we'd win.) Kids and adults both love it, and it's super easy to whip up.

Very Cherry Dessert Smoothie (9+)

This smoothie is in the dessert section because it's sweet, and your family will never have to know it's healthy. Your hands might get a little stained when you remove the cherry pits, but trust us, it's worth it.

INGREDIENTS:

1 cup pitted cherries

½ cup vanilla coconut or soy yogurt

½ cup frozen strawberries

½ cup unsweetened coconut milk

1 tsp. hemp oil

METHOD:

1. Combine all ingredients in blender and purée until smooth.
2. Throw in a little ice if you want a more frozen treat.
3. Pour into a mason jar, throw on a slouchy beanie and some flannel, and be a "sipster" with your baby.

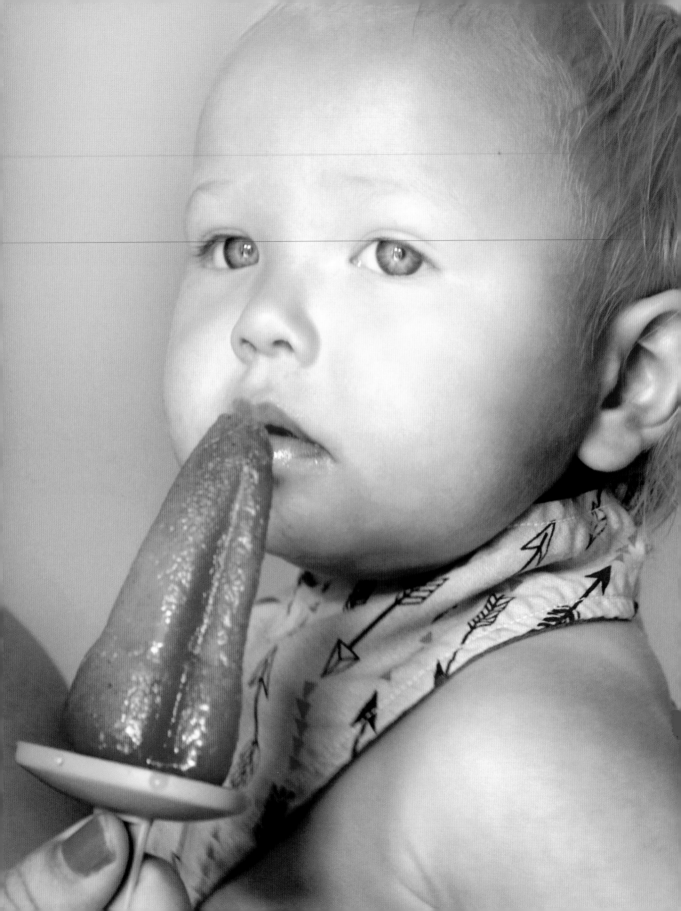

Watermelon Pops (9+)

These frozen treats are a perfectly pure and delicious choice for the whole fam. You'll probably have to sit your baby on your lap and help her with this one, but she'll love you for it.

INGREDIENTS:

1 cup watermelon, chopped

1 peach, pitted

1 kiwi, peeled

½ cup strawberries, washed, tops removed

METHOD:

1. Combine all ingredients in blender and chop until combined with small chunks.
2. Pour into popsicle molds, insert sticks, and freeze overnight until solid.

Cocoa Banana Nice Cream (9+)

This is a great and healthy "ice cream" that you do not need a high powered blender to create.

INGREDIENTS:

2 bananas peeled, chopped, and frozen

1 tbsp. cocoa powder

1 tsp. pure maple syrup

METHOD:

1. Peel and chop bananas, then freeze overnight.
2. Take out of freezer and let thaw for about 15 minutes *just* before making.
3. Combine semi-frozen banana pieces, cocoa, and syrup in blender and purée until mixed well. (Bananas will slowly continue to thaw the more they're worked, making blending easier.)
4. Using a spatula, move into freezer-safe container and place back in freezer to firm up, about 30 minutes.
5. Use an ice cream scoop to serve.

TIP: Mix it up! Skip the cocoa and toss in fresh blueberries, raspberries, or small chunks of peach before blending.

Grilled Stone Fruit (9+)

This is a simple way to get creative with fruit while you're doing some summer grilling.

INGREDIENTS:

1 peach

1 nectarine

1 tbsp. coconut oil

Dash cinnamon

METHOD:

1. Cut stone fruits in half and remove pits.
2. Brush the exposed flesh with coconut oil and sprinkle with cinnamon.
3. Place fruit on the grill, oil-side down.
4. Grill until warm, about 10 minutes, then slice and serve.

Coconut Whip with Raspberry Chia Compote (9+)

Honestly, this dessert is to die for. It's definitely for the whole family, not just your baby. It's so good, we've served it at dinner parties—honestly.

INGREDIENTS:

1 can full-fat coconut milk

1 tbsp. pure maple syrup

4 tbsp. chia seeds

3 tbsp. smashed fresh raspberries

3 tbsp. Mighty Mango (page 102)

METHOD:

1. Flip can of coconut milk upside down and place in refrigerator overnight.
2. Remove can from fridge and turn right side up before opening with can opener.
3. Separate the fiber from the liquid, reserving the liquid for other recipes and purées.
4. Spoon the fiber into a chilled mixing bowl.
5. Add the syrup and whip with a mixer.
6. In a separate bowl, combine chia seeds, smashed raspberries, and mango purée. Allow to sit for 5 minutes, stir again, and allow to rest another 5 minutes.
7. Spoon whipped coconut cream into individual serving bowls and top with raspberry chia compote.

Caramelized 'Nanners (9+)

These bad boys really hold their heat, so it's very important that you cool them on the counter or in the refrigerator for a few minutes (and check them) before serving to your baby.

INGREDIENTS:

1 banana, peeled

1 tbsp. coconut oil

½ tsp. cinnamon

METHOD:

1. Slice banana into half-inch-thick rounds.
2. Melt coconut oil in cast-iron skillet over medium heat.
3. Place banana rounds all around pan, being careful not to overlap.
4. Sprinkle with cinnamon and fry until golden. Carefully flip rounds over and fry the other side until golden as well.
5. Allow to cool to room temperature before serving.

Natural Remedies

We included these final few pages because we've both found ourselves, on several occasions, wishing for more holistic alternatives to conventional medicine for our babies' minor health issues. Neither of us have ever been comfortable with administering commercial pain relievers to our small children, and currently, there are few medications available for relief of colds and flus for children under the age of two. The following recipes are meant to fill that age gap, as well as provide natural relief for common baby and toddler complaints, such as colds, flus, teething, constipation, and diarrhea.

It's important to note that neither of us are trained in herbal medicine. Research used for writing *The Good Living Guide to Medicinal Tea* was recycled here, and we consulted a medicinal herbalist on a few of the recipes. If you have any hesitation about trying herbs in place of commercial medication, we urge you to consult an herbalist or naturopath.

Feel better, baby!

Chamomile Teething Treats (6+)

Chamomile is an all-natural soothing pain reliever, and it's super safe for all ages. It's also a mild sedative and is antibacterial and anti-inflammatory.[ix] One tea bag is generally equal to one tablespoon of dried herbs, so if you want to get really homemade and creative, you can grow, dry, and create your own tea bags with organic chamomile from your garden. (Friendly, non-bleached empty tea pouches can be purchased online or sometimes at your local health-food store. Ask around.) If you have a tea infuser handy, you can use that for making tea, following the one-tablespoon-equals-one-tea-bag rule.

Also, if your baby is really little and too young to suck on frozen treats, you can make a very strong pot of organic chamomile tea, allow it to cool to room temperature, then place it in your fridge until cold. Then, take a clean wash-cloth, soak it in the mixture, wring it out, and let your baby teethe on the cold cloth full of chamomile goodness.

INGREDIENTS:

2 cups filtered water
2 organic chamomile tea bags
1 tsp. organic brown rice syrup
6–8 small popsicle molds (depends on size)

METHOD:

1. Heat water until hot.
2. Add tea bags and steep for 15 minutes.
3. Remove bags and gently stir in syrup.
4. Allow to cool, then pour into popsicle molds and freeze.
5. Once frozen, remove from molds and let your baby suck and teethe on the treats, limiting her to two treats per day.

Tea Thyme for Cold + Flu (6+)

Until your children are at least two years old (usually closer to six), there are few over-the-counter commercial preparations that are deemed safe to administer when your children are ill. And let's be honest: with all that artificial coloring and flavoring and gelatin and other weird stuff, who wants to use it anyway?

Fortunately for you (and your baby!), thyme is a very effective cold and flu remedy. It's antibacterial, antiviral, and antiseptic. Unfortunately, it's also very pungent and flavorful, and many wee ones are put off by the taste. To help take away the bite of this tea, we dilute it and add maple syrup. The goal is to get your little one to drink one tablespoon, two times a day, throughout the duration of her cold. (Older children can drink more.)

INGREDIENTS:

2 cups filtered cold water
2 tbsp. freshly dried thyme
1 tsp. pure maple syrup

METHOD:

1. Heat 1 cup water until hot.
2. Add thyme and let steep for 10 minutes.
3. Strain herbs from water, add the last cup of water (cold), and stir in syrup. (Don't worry if there are tiny herb remnants in water.)
4. Give 1 tablespoon to your baby (we like to use clean medicinal syringes), twice per day, until her cold or flu visibly improves.

Break-a-Fever Pop (12+)

One of the most effective fever-reducers is probably sitting in your fridge right now. Lemon is a natural fever-reducer, detoxifier, and also very antibacterial.[x] When offered in the form of a frozen treat, it performs double duty because the lemony coldness will also help to soothe a hot little head. Make these at the beginning of cold and flu season (October), and keep them handy through-out the fall and winter.

Honey is included in this recipe, so it's only for babies over the age of twelve months. BUT—you can swap the honey for brown rice syrup, and then serve to a younger baby.

INGREDIENTS:

Juice and rind from one fresh lemon
2 cups filtered cold water
1 tbsp. pure honey
6–8 small popsicle molds (depends on size)

METHOD:

1. Combine juice, rind, and water. Mix well.
2. Add honey and whisk until smooth and well-blended.
3. Pour into popsicle molds and freeze thoroughly.
4. Serve to your baby, as much as she wants.

Soothing Lavender Water (6+)

Lavender is naturally calming and soothing and makes for a great bedtime experience. Many large cosmetic companies (such as Johnson & Johnson) know this and have marketed it expensively as a sleep aid for babies—they have a whole line of lavender baby products, including lotions, shampoos, and bubble bath.

We wanted to offer a very clean, holistic way to get lavender to work for you and your baby. In addition to purchasing pure essential oil and adding a couple of drops to your baby's bath or organic, scent-free lotions, you can make this lovely hydrating drink. (Again, if you want to use freshly dried organic lavender from your garden, do it—it'll smell and taste wonderful. And if you want to use a tea infuser, just follow the one-tablespoon-equals-one-tea-bag rule.)

INGREDIENTS:

2 organic lavender tea bags
2 cups filtered cold water

METHOD:

1. Steep tea bags in cold water in fridge for 30 minutes.
2. Remove tea bags and offer your baby up to ¼ cup before nap or bedtime, by way of medicinal dropper, bottle, or cup.

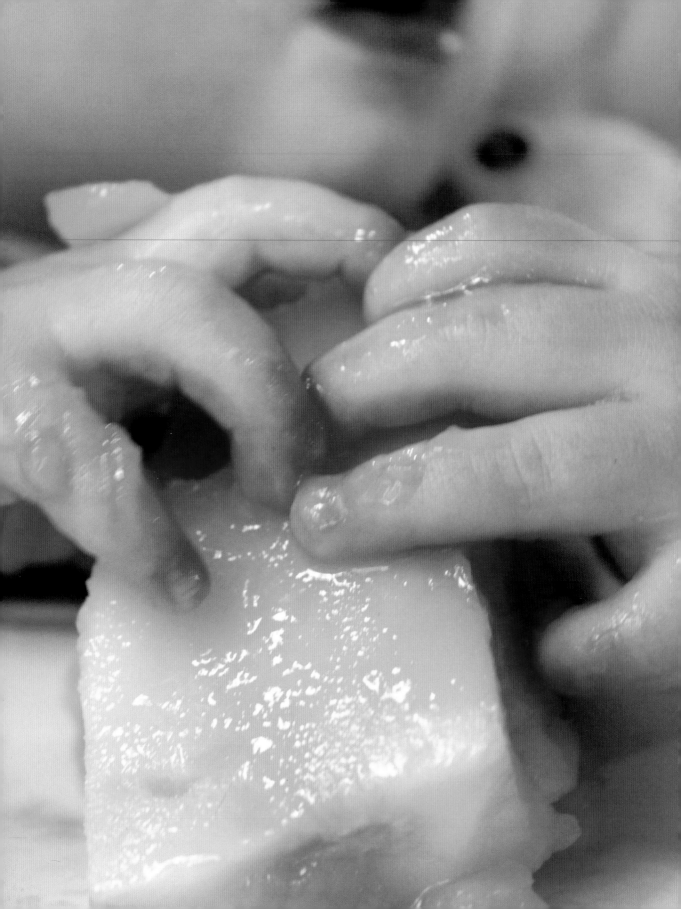

Mango Teether (6+)

Okay, so this one's not exactly a recipe. But pay attention because it's a great idea and it works really well!

When you're making a mango purée, save those big pits! As long as the pit is larger than your baby's mouth, you can freeze the pit and provide your baby with a sanity-saving teething treat.

*Babies should be supervised at all times while eating . . . or, um, gnawing.

Gluten-Free Lactation Cookies

Aside from dark, hoppy beer (which does work, but means you have to consume alcohol), there are a few ways to help induce lactation. These cookies are one of those ways.

INGREDIENTS:

¾ cup almond butter or seed butter
2 eggs
¼ cup coconut oil
1 tbsp. pure vanilla extract
½ cup flaxseeds
2 tbsp. ground brewer's yeast
1 ¾ cups gluten-free rolled oats
½ cup coconut crystals
1 tsp. aluminum-free baking soda
¼ cup slivered almonds
¼ cup chopped cashews

METHOD:

1. Preheat oven to 350°F.
2. Combine almond butter, eggs, coconut oil, and vanilla extract. Set aside.
3. Toss flaxseeds into blender and grind until crumbly.
4. If necessary, break down yeast until powdery with mortar and pestle.
5. Thoroughly combine almond butter mixture with flaxseeds, yeast, oats, coconut crystals, and baking soda.
6. Stir in almond slivers and cashew pieces.
7. Line a baking sheet with parchment paper and spray with a bit of coconut oil. Roll dough into balls and place on greased parchment paper.
8. Bake for 15 minutes. Happy nursing!

Happy Baby Teething Biscuits (9+)

Once your baby is old enough to teethe on a cookie (usually around 9 months), this recipe will be one of your favorites.

INGREDIENTS:

1½ cups gluten-free flour
½ cup coconut or almond flour
½ cup pure maple syrup
¼ cup unsweetened coconut milk
3 tbsp. blackstrap molasses
4 tbsp. coconut oil
1½ tbsp. pure vanilla extract

METHOD:

1. Preheat oven to 250°F.
2. Combine all ingredients in mixer using heavy paddle attachment. (Don't use a metal whisk attachment—this dough is dense and will damage it.)
3. Mix well, scraping sides of bowl every so often.
4. Flour counter and rolling pin and roll dough until it's a half-inch thick.
5. Using a knife, cut dough into rectangular slabs, about 1"x2" in size.
6. Bake for 2 hours, allowing the biscuits to get dry and hard, so your baby can really chew on them without pieces breaking off.
7. Cool completely before serving and store extra cookies in freezer.

Mellow Nettle Treats (9+)

We came up with this one when Otis had a reaction to the measles vaccine. He broke out in full-body hives, and although doctors prescribed him Benadryl for his itchy and painful rash, Tanya and I both felt like there had to be something kinder to his little body than commercial preparations.

This remedy is fantastic for rashes, seasonal allergies, sunburns, and an extra iron boost.

INGREDIENTS:

2 cups filtered water
2 organic nettle tea bags
1 tbsp. organic brown rice syrup
6–8 small popsicle molds (depends on size)

METHOD:

1. Heat water and steep tea bags for 15 minutes.
2. Remove tea bags and add syrup. Stir until thoroughly mixed.
3. Let cool, then pour into popsicle molds and freeze.
4. Once frozen, offer to your baby, limiting her to two treats per day.

TIP: Although many people associate nettle with stinging, recipes containing nettle will not sting you. As a precaution, we recommend not foraging your own nettle for this recipe; you can buy nettle leaf tea at your local health food store. (Traditional Medicinals is a great brand.)

Slow Your Roll—For When Things Get Crappy (6+)

This recipe can be served to your baby up to three times a day. Once the loose stool subsides, stop serving it—you don't want to go from one extreme to the other.

INGREDIENTS:

1 banana
½ cup applesauce
2 tbsp. gluten-free steel cut oats

METHOD:

1. Combine all ingredients in a blender and purée until smooth.
2. Serve immediately.

Moving Right Along Poop Inducer (6+)

You can feed this to your little one in conjunction with her regular baby food to help get things moving again.

INGREDIENTS:

2 pitted prunes
¼ cup fresh blueberries
2 tbsp. coconut milk yogurt or soy yogurt

METHOD:

Combine all ingredients in a blender and purée until smooth.

Recipe Index

LUNCH + DINNER

NATURAL REMEDIES

About the Authors

Jennifer Browne has been writing books about health and wellness since 2011. Having experienced many food sensitivities herself, she's well-versed in making mindful choices and using food as medicine. Passionate about food sustainability and responsibility, this self-proclaimed hippie chick lives with her husband and three crazy kids just outside of Vancouver, BC. *Baby Nosh* is her fourth book; other books by Browne include *Happy Healthy Gut, Vegetarian Comfort Foods,* and *The Good Living Guide to Medicinal Tea.*

Visit her website at jenniferbrowne.org, or tweet her @jennifer_browne.

Photo by Cristal Sawatzky of Level 6 Images

Tanya R. Loewen is a Vancouver-based photographer, tattoo artist, and mom-bot. She can be found adventuring, gardening, or wasting time by the ocean with her husband and four rambunctious children. After the birth of her youngest, Otis, she overhauled the way she ate and fed her family to accommodate his dietary sensitivities. She feels it's important that kids grow up understanding what food is and where it comes from before it hits the local grocer or farmer's market. The daughter of a farmer and a devoted gardener, she has always had a strong sense of pride when it comes to the growing and maintenance of crops and plants, be it urban or rural, as well as eating healthy from the ground up. Since venturing into commercial photography, she has photographed several published books. This is the first she has co-authored.

Visit her website at wildhoneyarthouse.com.

References

[i] "Food." *Merriam-Webster Online Dictionary*. Web. 2015. http://www.merriam-webster.com/dictionary/food

[ii] Michael K. Georgieff. "Does My Baby Need an Iron Supplement?" *Baby Center*. Web. 2015. http://www.babycenter.com/404_does-my-baby-need-an-iron-supplement_1334529.bc

[iii] James T. C. Li, M.D., Ph.D. "What's the difference between a food intolerance and food allergy?" *The Mayo Clinic*. Web. 2014. http://www.mayoclinic.org/diseases-conditions/food-allergy/expert-answers/food-allergy/faq-20058538

[iv] "Calcium in Plant-Based Diets." *Physicians Committee for Responsible Medicine*. Web. 2015. http://pcrm.org/health/diets/vsk/vegetArian-starter-kit-calcium

[v] "National Organic Program." *The United States Department of Agriculture*. Web. 2015. http://www.ams.usda.gov/AMSv1.0/NOPOrganicStandards

[vi] *The David Suzuki Foundation*. Web. 2015. http://www.davidsuzuki.org/what-you-can-do/queen-of-green/faqs/food/what-are-the-dirty-dozen-and-the-clean-fifteen/

[vii] Dr. Mark Hyman. "5 Reasons High Fructose Corn Syrup Will Kill You." *DrHyman.com*. Web. 2014. http://drhyman.com/blog/2011/05/13/5-reasons-high-fructose-corn-syrup-will-kill-you/

[viii] "Potato plant poisoning - green tubers and sprouts." *Medline Plus*. Web. 2013. http://www.nlm.nih.gov/medlineplus/ency/article/002875.htm

[ix] Janmejai K. Srivastava, Eswar Shankar, and Sanjay Gupta. "Chamomile: A herbal medicine of the past with bright future." *Pubmed*. Web. 2010. http://www.ncbi.nlm.nih.gov/pmc/articles/PMC2995283/

[x] "Lemons (Fruit)." *Herb Wisdom*. Web. 2015. http://www.herbwisdom.com/herb-lemon.html